Brenda CampbellJones, Shannon Keeny, ... have creatively expanded the expectati(... ..sation for establishing a more equitable society. It is a clear call to improve relationships in ways that are practical, engaging, and inspiring.

The authors take us beyond conversations on race, class, and culture to alignment with our inner core via asking and answering difficult questions. Finally, a conversation that can be held... honestly.

Dr. Theresa Saunders
Associate Professor, Education Leadership and Counseling,
Eastern Michigan University; Consultant, African American Student Initiative,
Michigan Department of Education

. . . .

This book is not just read—it is "lived." The authors challenge and encourage each reader to be a mindful participant in a dynamic conversation of life. Individual voices carry the potential of the heart while our collective voices have unmatched power to liberate the dormant power of human potential.

Richard S. Martinez, EdD
Diversity Consultant, Leadership Coach, Founder of the Artful Alliance

. . . .

Instead of pathologizing and exploiting differences, the authors offer core components of meaningful conversation about the real and often-divisive issues that emerge from the power dynamics implicit within diversity. They teach us how to engage with each other in a way that honors dignity, affirms personhood, and builds community.

John Krownapple
Diversity, Equity, and Inclusion Coordinator, Howard County, Maryland

. . . .

As we have deeper conversations beyond race, class, and cultural boundaries, this book inspires readers to pose questions that "open up what is possible rather than shut down the emergence of newness."

I am inspired to reflect on why I teach, how I communicate and cocreate with all members of the learning community, and what I need to do to expand my capacity to communicate truthfully and freely on behalf of the students and families that I serve.

Alicia S. Monroe, EdD
Career Expert & Adjunct Professor, Rowan University; ASCD Faculty;
CEO/Founder, Solutions for Sustained Success, LLC

CULTURE, CLASS, and RACE

BRENDA
CampbellJones

SHANNON
Keeny

FRANKLIN
CampbellJones

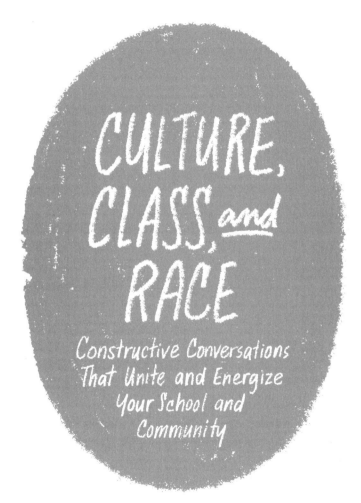

CULTURE, CLASS, and RACE

Constructive Conversations
That Unite and Energize
Your School and
Community

Alexandria, Virginia USA

1703 N. Beauregard St. • Alexandria, VA 22311-1714 USA
Phone: 800-933-2723 or 703-578-9600 • Fax: 703-575-5400
Website: www.ascd.org • E-mail: member@ascd.org
Author guidelines: www.ascd.org/write

Ranjit Sidhu, *Executive Director and CEO;* Stefani Roth, *Publisher;* Genny Ostertag, *Director, Content Acquisitions;* Susan Hills, *Senior Acquisitions Editor;* Julie Houtz, *Director, Book Editing & Production;* Darcie Russell, *Senior Associate Editor;* Judi Connelly, *Senior Art Director;* Donald Ely, *Associate Art Director;* Valerie Younkin, *Senior Production Designer;* Kelly Marshall, *Interim Manager, Production Services;* Trinay Blake, *E-Publishing Specialist;* Isel Pizarro, *Senior Production Specialist*

All web links in this book are correct as of the publication date below but may have become inactive or otherwise modified since that time. If you notice a deactivated or changed link, please e-mail books@ascd.org with the words "Link Update" in the subject line. In your message, please specify the web link, the book title, and the page number on which the link appears.

PAPERBACK ISBN: 978-1-4166-2832-3   ASCD product #118010   n1/20

PDF E-BOOK ISBN: 978-1-4166-2834-7; see Books in Print for other formats.

Quantity discounts are available: e-mail programteam@ascd.org or call 800-933-2723, ext. 5773, or 703-575-5773. For desk copies, go to www.ascd.org/deskcopy.

Library of Congress Cataloging-in-Publication Data is available for this title.

Library of Congress Control Number: 2019038546

30 29 28 27 26 25 24 23 22 21 20   1 2 3 4 5 6 7 8 9 10 11 12

To future generations of children yet to be born. It is my expectation that the conversations we have today will lead to a world of justice and celebration for who you are born to be—exceptional human beings.
—Brenda CampbellJones

. . . .

To my parents and those who came before them. The love, encouragement, and guidance they showered upon me continue to drive me. To everyone who has been brave enough to share their story with me, I am forever changed because of you. I ask you to continue to tell your story and listen to others tell theirs.
—Shannon Keeny

. . . .

To our children, grandchildren, and great-grandchildren, who mirror all children in society. This book is intended to stimulate conversation with the potential of maintaining and advancing equity in schools, neighborhoods, and society.
—Franklin CampbellJones

Foreword

Our society, as well as esteemed members of our profession, have difficulty discussing issues of equity, let alone potentially more combustible topics such as "inequities." Drawing from their extensive research, academic training, and on-the-ground experiences in preK-12 schools, the authors seek to demystify and "demythify" these topics by offering field-tested approaches, strategies, and activities. Every educator—whether a first-year teacher or an experienced teacher, counselor, or administrator—can gain valuable professional knowledge and insights that will ultimately benefit all students academically and socially.

This professional learning experience, shared in the pages of this book, seeks to break barriers of inequity. It is about providing students in our schools access to the ideals of a democratic society. The authors provide ways to assess

- Your comfort and skills in conversations that involve issues of equity.
- Your knowledge and understanding of issues related to educational inequities.

At the end of each chapter, the authors provide activities that are specifically designed to guide your personal learning and reflections and to serve as dialogic strategies that you can use in your professional learning communities.

One thing comes through clearly in this book: conversations do matter! The authors have captured the essence of why conversations matter when the topic is about -isms, including racism, sexism, classism, and ableism. These topics and other learned treatments of people as a result of systemic oppression are typically avoided or often result in anger, denial, stuckness, and even broken relationships. This well-curated text gives educators guidance for engaging in intentional and meaningful conversations about the best ways to relate to each other, including step-by-step practical plans and strategies for thinking together, even when their points of view and life experiences differ.

Early in the book you will find definitions of vocabulary terms often used in conversations about diversity but rarely understood through a common frame or common experiences. The definitions have emerged through understandings developed through dialogue, research, and shared experiences. Too often school leaders make decisions about access to resources, lack of resources, and abundances without shared understanding of important terms that are basic to education, such as *inequity, disproportionality, disparity,* and *equality* versus *equity.* Without such understanding, leaders often make decisions in isolation from the marginalized, disenfranchised, and silenced individuals for whom the decisions are being made. Shared visioning, decision making, resources, and opportunities rarely happen without first engaging in mindful and intentional dialogue that is needed to develop shared understanding of these terms and those who do and those who do not benefit from them. Using the guidance offered, facilitators and participants alike will learn the intricacies and highly prized skills involved in true dialogue.

It's All About Trust and Relationships

Margaret Wheatley, scientist and systems thinker, describes organizations by using the metaphor of living, breathing systems (Wheatley, 2009). Systems must be nurtured and energized for growth. They do not depend on hierarchy and organizational charts. They do depend on growth processes and energy exchanges and interactions. These interactions lead to connections and relationships. Wheatley says that for growth to occur, organizations must pay attention to

- Their vision and identity;

- The information that flows throughout the organization; and, most important,
- The relationships.

The authors emphasize the importance of relational trust among members of schools and organizations that serve diverse student populations and are confronting issues surrounding and including lack of access and inequity. After all, schools are composed of people learning and working together. Without trust, teachers are suspicious of decisions administrators make, parents are reluctant to believe what teachers and leaders say about how decisions and rules are made, and administrators might hesitate to implement board policies when the only response to the question "Why do we do it this way?" is "We've always done it this way." Without trust, the organization loses energy, lacks nurturing, and suffers from loss.

The Power of Questions for Transformative Action

Powerful questions can change the way people think. Some questions can cause educators to shut down their thinking and refuse to engage further in a conversation about some demographic groups. Consider this example: "Why do we always have to focus on those kids? Do you actually think they can do this work and graduate?" Responses to this and similar questions range from people leaving the room to others arguing with the questioner: "Sure, they can. Just because you can't teach them doesn't mean they can't make it. Have a little sympathy, will ya?"

These questions and comments are barriers and do not support thinking. Well-crafted, nonjudgmental, open-ended questions can prompt new ways of thinking that actually break down the barriers. Powerful and breakthrough questions (Lindsey, Jungwirth, Pahl, & Lindsey, 2009) use a protocol for framing action to mediate thinking. In this book, the reader is led through the protocol, learning how to enable new ways of staying in the conversation and to spur transformative action.

How Stories Help Us Connect at New Levels

Stories connect us. In her book *Storycatcher*, Christina Baldwin (2005) says:

> Story—the abundance of it, and the lack of it—shapes us. Story—the abundance of it, the lack of it—gives us place, lineage, history, a sense of self.... The power of story is understood by the powerful, yet the power of story belongs to all of us, especially the least powerful. History is what scholars and conquerors say happened; story is what it was like to live on the ground. (pp. 3–4)

Storytelling is also a powerful resource in this book. In some cases you will relate to the narrator and say, "That happened to me, too." Other times you may read the story and think, "How could that happen? Why would it still be happening today?" As educators we must be willing to ask each other, "What is your story? What do I need to know? What would you like me to know?" The purpose of asking these questions of each other is so we can learn together.

Baldwin (2005) says, "Not every word that comes out of our mouths is a story. Story is a narrative. Words are how we think; narrative is how we link" (p. 10). The authors of this book use story to link critical terms and definitions and to enable readers to learn new concepts through different experiences, via the Try This exercises. Clearly, *Culture, Class, and Race: Constructive Conversations That Unite and Energize Your School and Community* is a book about developing trust, relationships, and conversations that lead to understanding the importance of how race, class, and culture intersect. These intersections affect our identity, our values, our beliefs, and our assumptions. Mindful conversations help educators clarify and unify their efforts so that more students know who they are in this complex world.

Delores B. Lindsey, retired associate professor,
California State University–San Marcos

Randall B. Lindsey, emeritus professor,
California State University–Los Angeles

1
Prepare to Engage

Racial affiliation, gender identification, social stratification, and ethnicity are conversational minefields where few people choose to venture. After 25 years' experience in guiding educators through these difficult conversations, we are sharing tangible, practical advice on how to explore these traditionally taboo topics on your own and with your colleagues. We write about these topics with direct and simple language that, in turn and with practice, will enable you and your colleagues to discuss them as you build community.

Although these topics are complex, we are guided by the philosophy that complexity is built from multiple simple components. And, beginning by discussing simple or basic components frees us to explore our common ill-informed understanding and ignorance and generate connections for future collaborations. More immediate, we want you to be confident when engaging in meaningful conversation about societal challenges surrounding the power dynamics founded upon classifications of race, gender, and class, and the many other excuses and reasons used for misunderstandings that fragment society and disrupt civil community.

We apply these key principles to our work and suggest that you use them to guide your conversations:

- Understanding our values and beliefs is key to knowing ourselves and why we do what we do. In knowing how we come to understand, we begin to know how others understand as well.
- Listening with empathy is important. Listening to others informs our ability to empathize with people who are thought to be different from us. Empathy further expands self-knowledge and fortifies trust within a community.
- Promoting belongingness and focusing on developing healthy relationships between and among us is both needed and wanted.
- Engaging authentically with one another requires developing skills to do so—and using them. We do not live alone.

Read with Purpose

As an educator, you know that thinking about your intentions for reading—reading with purpose—will help you focus your learning and memory. And, one good pre-reading routine is to raise self-reflective questions about what you are going to read. Ask yourself several key questions:

- What are my assumptions about what I am going to read?
- What are my hopes for reading?
- What do I need to know about myself as I read?

We recommend the good practice of taking notes or keeping a journal. Sometimes you may be provoked in a way that reveals background information stowed deep within your life experience. Such revelation could provide insight as to your willingness or ability to respond to certain situations. Take notes about key ideas you want to remember. What spikes your curiosity may be the entry point to exciting self-discoveries and lead to knowledge of others. What ideas are discussed that are in alignment with your core beliefs? What ideas do not align with the way you self-identify? How might this book relate to you as a person and a professional?

Reading this book is an active learning experience that we hope will engage you and help you to involve others in a commitment to equity. Our hope is that it will help you to raise questions, generate ideas or new ways of thinking, and ignite your courage to have conversations of great meaning that change the culture of schools, social interactions, and larger community environments.

Practice

You will find a Try This section in each chapter. The activities within have been carefully selected and designed to promote and support your exploration of key ideas. In many cases, a deeper experiential dive into a topic will help you grasp the simple understandings within the complex topic. Reading this book and using the questions and activities will assist you—and your colleagues, if applicable—in developing neural pathways for processing and behaving differently. These experiences can help make connections and further unpack experiences and concepts over time and can help integrate these thoughts and learning into daily life.

As humans, we aspire to social engagement and connection with our community. Through social engagement, we generate, negotiate, and renegotiate experiences to make sense of what we learn and do. Share with your colleagues what you learn and how you react as you read and participate in the activities. If possible, read this book along with colleagues and use the activities to share experiences and have larger, better-informed conversations.

Summon Courage

As attributed to ancient Chinese philosopher and writer Lao Tzu, "Being deeply loved by someone gives you strength, while loving someone deeply gives you courage." On those grounds, everyone has courage—though it may be a challenge to summon it when most needed. Today, our capacity to be courageous is smothered under a cloak of political correctness given the highly volatile space where relationships coalesce. The toxicity is so pervasive that it has permeated our homes and private encampments. Some of the most contentious conversations reportedly occur at traditional family gatherings, even Thanksgiving. Even in these personal spaces and under special conditions, or perhaps because of them, summoning courage is necessary.

When we view courage as a muscle, we gain a sense of how courage development might work. As with the muscle, your courage gains strength when used regularly. We also recognize that it shrinks and weakens when not used. But what is courage? How do we describe it?

Courage: 1. the attitude of facing and dealing with anything recognized as dangerous, difficult, or painful, instead of withdrawing from it; quality of being fearless or brave, valor. 2. mind; purpose; spirit (*Merriam-Webster Dictionary*, May 5, 2019).

We easily understand the first part of the definition as it captures the essence of heroes and heroines in books and movies. As for the second, we believe mind, purpose, and spirit are embodied within a person's heart or *cor*. The temperament for brave action rises from within and offers us strength for acts of valor. It is *cor* that enables a person's action in the instance or instances of adversity. We encourage you to reach into your *cor* and summon courage—courage to have conversations that cross cultural borders, social status lines, and gender-specific assignments. Our intent is to help you and your colleagues follow Lao Tzu's lead to love yourself and your neighbor enough to engage in conversations that harness the potential to bind us rather than to split us apart.

These conversations take effort. If your experiences with these sorts of conversations were divisive or degenerated into shouting matches or tears, you may find it difficult to begin. If you are accustomed to generating critical conversations that lead to positive outcomes, you may embrace these opportunities. If you have been silent on many issues and feel disconnected from your community, take the opportunity to be heard and join in. Despite your experience, the risk of *not* engaging overshadows the risk of pursuit. Disengaging in a space where your participation is needed withholds an important perspective that could inform the action of the entire community. Your voice matters.

Prepare to Engage

It is our experience that members of the education community—including students, teachers, counselors, psychologists, administrators, parents, and board members—want to connect with one another beyond societal norms. Within or across these groupings, however, conversations about gender assignments, racial identity, social classification, and ethnic affiliation are often considered dangerous to the point of being unapproachable. Connecting across all these identities or affinity groups (real and imagined, personal and professional) requires engagement and purposeful conversation along with an exchange of ideas that reach into our individual experiences, which are unique to our background knowledge or lifeworld. The act of authentically sharing our lifeworld experiences has the potential of unveiling the imaginary differences that divide us into affinity groups. Sharing who you are and your unique experiences and perceptions allows others to enter and experience the world as you do. Stripping away the illusion of separation frees us to see and explore the many nearby pitfalls and entrapments as we learn to eviscerate them from our conscious experience.

With free-flowing purposeful conversation, interconnected relationships are possible. Many school environments, however, function as conversational deserts with sparse dialogues, malnourished relationships, and withered communities. Conversationally famished educators come to our workshops and eagerly break their silence, participate in active discourse, and share their lifeworld. They frequently express fulfillment after a day of productive exchange centered on race, class, sexual orientation, and culture.

We find that conversations that flourish and are free-flowing share the following attributes.

- We love to share our stories. An exchange of struggles, concerns, and joy is a way of connecting and discovering how similar we are.
- We like to feel unimpeded when sharing elements of truth. Our personal perception is truth, at least until we hear more information or different truths. Sharing multiple versions of a story or truth gives us perspective and allows us to be open to hearing and seeing from other points of view. To be open to other points of view

is our primary orientation of expression. Consider the metaphor of a flower unfolding as it blooms to people "opening up" to communicate and exchange ideas.

- We enjoy consensus. The more we agree with one another, the more stable and confident we are in our lifeworld. The more confident we become, the more certain we are of the actions we take.
- We negotiate the perceived shared space among us. Learning the ground rules is essential, especially when cultivating new terrain around traditions perceived to threaten our lifeworld experiences.
- We believe trust is fundamental to communication. Without trust, communication breaks down and relationships are dysfunctional.

We discuss these attributes and highlight their importance in creating healthy relationships. They help us disconnect from unhealthy associations with race, class, and culture. Our intent is to establish a platform for your engagement in healthy relationships beyond these outdated affinity groups.

Begin with a Story

We draw from our vast experience as equity facilitators working with schools and community organizations in the United States and Canada. We share our proven techniques for facilitating sensitive critical conversations and nurturing relationships. Just as important, we share stories of individuals who are traversing the journey of eviscerating oppressive behaviors and traditions from their personal and professional lives. Stories matter. We honor the years of stories shared by people who have wrestled with challenges that were presented by an illusion of separation. Their stories and insights provide richness and depth to our work. We anticipate that your experience with these topics will be confirmed and challenged, ultimately adding to the richness of your perspective and expanding your horizon of the human experience.

We use different formats to convey our key concepts. The stories, poems, reflections, and activities can help you find the materials needed to construct new meanings and forge better ideas that fit your community. The stories are from our own experiences and from the experiences of colleagues who gave us permission to share with you. We invite you to consider your own story in similar situations, whenever appropriate. We begin with Shannon's story.

Shannon's Story

My home is in Baltimore, Maryland. Of the many things that define Baltimore—poets, musicians, history—it is noted most often for the crime rate (an average of one murder each day in 2017). My city has the third largest police force in the United States and remains divided both racially and economically. As a white female in a historically white neighborhood, I feel very comfortable and safe in my community and in my three-level row home with a rooftop deck. Here is an experience that I'd like to share.

On a clear January day with sun shining and the temperature about 60°F, I decided to sit on my rooftop deck and disconnect from my busy work life. With no phone and no company, I knew at the click of the door that I'd locked myself out. Somewhat bemused, I wondered how I was going to get back inside.

My first idea was to break the glass door with the table on my deck. When that didn't work, I climbed over the railing to the adjacent home. Three railings and decks later, I still did not have success—no one was home to hear me knock on the windows or cry out for help. Panic came over me as I wondered what I would do if I couldn't get inside.

In desperation, I looked down and spotted a man on the sidewalk. I yelled to get his attention. When he looked up, I said, "Please help me— I am locked out of my house." He looked shocked when I pointed to my house (three rooftops away) and said, "I live there." He asked if it would be helpful to call the police for assistance. I insisted that he climb the fence to my backyard and enter the unlocked back door. He agreed. Within a few minutes he climbed the fence, entered my house, climbed the three flights of stairs, tracked through my bedroom, and opened the deck door. Hooray! I was free. With laughter and a sigh of relief, I hugged him and thanked him from the bottom of my heart for having rescued me. He was my hero!

After seeing him off, I sat down on my couch and began to laugh and then cry. I called my parents and said, "Don't worry, I am OK." Of course, they had no idea what had happened, so I explained. They laughed and agreed that I had created quite the story.

Two days later, I took an emotional pivot. My joy at being rescued waned as a troubling reality entered my consciousness. As I traced the event from start to finish, I was saddened by the many times the story could have ended tragically. If I were a black female, would I have attempted to break the glass on my own door? Would I have climbed my neighbors' railings, walked across their decks, and knocked on their windows? Would I have called to a stranger from a neighbor's deck and asked him to enter my house to rescue me? Would it have mattered if the rescuer was white or black? Male or female?

These questions and more flooded my mind. What was most disturbing is that I did not think about any of these problems at the time. Why? As a white female, I am nearly oblivious to the perils that people of color face every day. I did not consider that anyone would be concerned about me climbing over railings to neighbors' rooftops or that anyone would call the police to report me as a thief. I felt completely justified in trying to break into my own house. At that moment, I realized that my whiteness meant something. It gave me the privilege and the confidence to climb on roofs, knock on third-story doors, and demand the help that I needed. In a moment of reflection, I felt both guilt and anger: Guilt because race isn't something I think about every moment of every day. Anger because other people have to think about race every moment of every day.

I thought of Dr. Henry Louis Gates Jr., prominent scholar at Harvard University, creator and host of many PBS movies and film projects, and author of many books and journal publications. His front door jammed and Gates was arrested for breaking into his own house. The police questioned Gates about his proper identity and residence. Despite attempts to prove his identity, he was taken to jail on charges of disorderly conduct. The charges were later dropped (Thompson, 2009).

I thought of Lolade Siyonbola, an African American student who fell asleep while completing papers for her master's degree. A white student reported her to the campus police as an "unauthorized person" in the dorm. She was questioned by police, who told her, "we need to make sure you belong here" (Caron, 2018).

I remembered Rashon Nelson and Donte Robinson, two African American men arrested within 10 minutes of entering a Philadelphia coffee house while waiting to meet a friend to discuss a potential business investment. Their reported crime was "not ordering drinks and refusing to leave." Charges were later dropped and the CEO apologized in an open letter to the public (Whack, 2018).

I thought of these events and wondered about all the ones that I didn't hear about. I'm convinced these sorts of events happen daily. I felt anger that these atrocities occur and guilt because I have the privilege not to think of them at all.

Try This   Exploring Your Cultural Identity

We often associate with our sociocultural identities, including race, class, ethnic background, gender affiliation, religion, occupation, and sexual orientation. In Shannon's Story, Shannon later realized that her experience could have been different, depending on her race and gender affiliation. For this activity, explore how you might experience advantages or disadvantages related to one aspect of your cultural identity. Use the following exercise to remind yourself of a time when you experienced your identity and how the experience affected you.

1. Recall a story connected to one aspect of your social cultural identity (e.g., white, female, dad, soccer parent, or religious affiliation). Make a few notes about the story that connects with how that aspect of your identity affected the experience (who was there, where you were, and why the event was memorable).

2. Identify a trusted friend, family member, or colleague and share your social cultural identity and story. Ask your partner to do the same and share.

3. After you and your trusted friend, family member, or colleague have shared stories about your experiences, gather two or three other parties to engage in the same process (steps 1 and 2). We find it's best for you to offer your story and then allow everyone time to think and write. Give everyone the opportunity to share their experience in a dialogic setting. Below are some questions to consider when creating a safe and nurturing space for authentic sharing.

- What do members of the group need to feel safe while sharing?
- What are some ways that you would like the group to share their story? For example, round robin, in pairs, in group, or in a circle?
- What is a good location for sharing?
- Afterward, use the following prompts to guide your reflection on the activity.
  — What does this experience evoke in you?
  — What did you learn about yourself?
  — What did you learn about how groups share stories and listen to others sharing stories?
  — In what ways might you apply this learning?

2

Unite Around
Essential Terms

You can mandate behavioral changes in authoritarian, command-and-control cultures. People will behave in prescribed ways, but their behavior will be compliance behavior, in response to an external source of authority. Compliance will last only as long as force is applied. And force most often fuels resistance and reinforces the attitudes and beliefs that it seeks to change.

–Linda Ellinor and Glenna Gerard (1998, p. 222)

Many advocate for having courageous conversations about race (Ladson-Billings, 2016; Singleton, 2015; Singleton & Linton, 2006; Tatum, 2017), developing a deep understanding of the centrality of classism to maintain and advance poverty (Freire, 2000; Gorski, 2008), or gaining proficient skills to become culturally competent (Cross, 1989; Lindsey, Nuri-Robins, Terrell, & Lindsey, 2018).

To facilitate these worthy goals, it is essential that you willfully engage with others on an even platform using clear and appropriate terminology. Doing so ensures equal voice among participants, minimizing the power imbalances that can occur because of verbal advantage. We have observed, in many cases, dialogues that quickly spiral into debate marked with verbal and intellectual bullying, where some people with superior linguistic skills lay traps for those with lesser verbal skills. The result is conversation that is dominated by the biggest verbal bully on the block. We argue for accepting and opening horizons, which facilitates greater participation, particularly by voices often drowned out by fear.

For successful conversations, we need to have shared vocabulary. Deciding who establishes a definition is as important as the definition itself. It is our view that those participating in a group are best positioned to establish and extend definitions for group conversation. Consequently, it is essential that conversationalists entering cross-cultural relationships establish agreed-upon definitions for sharing intimate details of their lifeworld experiences. How you perceive and experience life through social assignments such as ability, race, sexual orientation, or class profoundly affects how you enter authentic conversations in cross-cultural spaces. Identifying and understanding the definitions of words that are being used gives each participant common tools and parameters to safely navigate the space and shorten the perceived distance among perspectives. Having the proper means to facilitate language use has the potential of enhancing shared understanding and ensures development of mutual perspectives.

The following terms and definitions are offered as an essential organizer for fruitful conversations. Common definitions of terms facilitates cross-fertilization of personal perspectives and group horizon expansion. As you read the proposed definitions, reflect on and compare the description with how you might use the term. Note whether the meaning given affirms, helps clarify, or challenges your thinking. The act of discerning your relationship to the definition given is as important as the actual use of the term. Links to related websites provide additional resources for your continued study. We encourage you to do research to stay abreast of the changes in these rapidly evolving definitions.

Ableism. Oppressive practices and dominant attitudes in society that devalue and limit the potential of people with perceived differences in abilities from those in the dominant group. Ableism is a set of practices and beliefs that assign inferior value (worth) to people who have special emotional, physical, or psychiatric needs. Ableist attitudes define these differences as inherently negative and assume that people with these perceived differences need to be "fixed." Individuals classified as having special needs through the practice of ableism are viewed as deviant, inferior, and burdensome. See the following sites for more information:

- http://cdrnys.org/blog/uncategorized/ableism/
- https://www.ada.gov/regs2010/titleIII_2010/titleIII_2010 _regulations.htm
- http://www.stopableism.org/p/what-is-ableism.html
- https://philosophycommons.typepad.com/disability_and _disadvanta/2018/10/cfp-ableism-in-the-academy-a-series-about -disability-oppression-and-resistance-in-higher-education.html

Cross-Cultural. *Cross-cultural* refers to intersections of cultural boundaries. Intersections provide moments to explore variations and similarities of cultural experiences held by groups. These crossover moments advance individual and group perspectives with the potential of expanding and deepening lifeworld reference points.

Culture. Values, assumptions, and beliefs that a group normalizes through their actions. Culture becomes the way things are consistently done, perhaps daily. It reflects the belief systems and behaviors informed by sociological factors like gender, age, sexual orientation, and physical ability. Over time, cultural behaviors become tradition that is handed down to the next generation.

Culture of Poverty. A myth based on the refuted research of Oscar Lewis's (1961) *The Children of Sanchez*. It is our experience both personally and professionally that people stricken with poverty are far from the caricatures placed upon them by Lewis's work. They are motivated and have strong work ethics and are involved in educating their children.

Paul Gorski (2008) provides an informed list of myths that characterize families stricken with poverty as lazy, drug abusers, and not valuing their child's education. Gorski's myths align with society's deep-seated belief in classism. According to Gorski, we shouldn't pay attention to the myths, but to the persistence of classism. The theory of classism clings to a deficit model that insists something is lacking within the individual or group that determines impoverished circumstances rather than persistent structural barriers that purposefully assigns them to a socioeconomic status. The practice of "redlining" is an example of one such structural barrier. After World War II, the Federal Housing Authority withheld funds from African Americans and Latinos, a practice that resulted in the unfair distribution of wealth among citizens. The consequences led to a rapid growth of wealth for some citizens classified as white at the expense of citizens classified as nonwhite. This structural gap in wealth persists today; the net worth of the average white family is 13 times greater than the net worth of the average black family (Thompson, 2018).

Cultural Proficiency. Highlights the most ideal point on the cultural competence continuum developed by Terry Cross (1989), in *Towards a Culturally Competent System of Care.* It describes the policies and practices of an organization, or the values and behaviors of an individual, that enable cultural proficiency in a way that reflects how an organization treats its employees, its clients, and its community. This is the point on the continuum wherein sits equity.

Diversity. *Diversity* is a general term for indicating that many people with many different traits are present in an organization or group. Closely associated with diversity is the term *multicultural*, referring to many cultures within the same grouping. Multicultural may refer to the sociodynamics of economics, power, privilege, class, ethnicity, race, language, gender, age, ability, or sexual orientation.

Equality. Equality speaks to equal treatment, or inputs, in the name of fairness based on the notion of a meritocracy. Regardless of social historical obstructions, this concept treats all people as the same without acknowledging differences such as age, gender, language, or ability. Equality without the practice of equity results in unfair, unequal outcomes that marginalize certain groups.

Equity. Equity speaks to the practice of fairness by ascribing to the realization "that the advancement of a small group cannot be achieved or sustained unless the larger population is allowed to share in the benefits" (Blankstein & Noguera, 2016, p. 60). Equitable programs make accommodations for differences so that the outcomes are the same for all individuals. The notion of equity challenges the belief in societal distribution of benefits. For example, some school districts give administrators and teachers five days of bereavement leave and noncertified personnel three days of bereavement leave. This is an unfair practice. Equality means everyone gets the same number of days. Equity means each person gets the number of days needed.

Inclusion. A term used to indicate that diverse groups and perspectives are purposely represented and embraced in all sectors of an organization and organizational life. Inclusion, in a society driven by exclusivity, results from intentional acts that go against the practice of privilege and entitlement for a few at the expense of many.

Politically Correct. A term used to describe language that reflects sensitivity to the diversity of a group, often without an understanding or caring about why such sensitivity is important. The intent of political correctness is to stay out of trouble. Politically correct responses are usually insincere and do not reflect an understanding of or concern for why a group makes a particular request (Lindsey et al., 2018, p. 166).

Race. A modern construct in human history. Race is a sociopolitical construct designed to divide populations based on certain biological features. In the United States and throughout the Americas, skin color is used as the determining factor for social and economic partitioning. Although race has no biological foundation, racism is real. For more information, see www.pbs.org/race.

Racism. Racism is a system of advantage based upon race (Wellman, 1993, cited in Tatum, 2017). In the United States and throughout the Americas, racial social advantage is given to people having the biological characteristic labeled white; people labeled of color are denied societal benefits based upon the amount of melanin in their body.

Religious Discrimination. Religious bigotry or intolerance involves the practice of discriminating based on religious identity. An oppressive practice, it seeks to exclude members of selected religious affiliations from enjoying full societal benefit. The civil rights laws enforced by the U.S. Department of Education's Office for Civil Rights (OCR) protect all students, regardless of religious identity, from discrimination on the basis of race, color, national origin, sex, disability, and age. For more information, see https://www2.ed.gov/about /offices/list/ocr/religion.html.

Sexual Identification. Sexual identification can be best described as a range of social and biological associations rather than a defined point. As a term with a wide range of possible groupings with emerging definitions, we suggest exploring several websites with detailed language before engaging in difficult conversations. Use these websites to begin your understanding:

- https://www.plannedparenthood.org/learn/sexual-orientation -gender/sexual-orientation
- http://www.welcomingschools.org/resources/definitions /definitions-for-adults/
- https://www.lgbt.ucla.edu/

Tolerance. Resentful acceptance of differences with which a person disagrees or is unfamiliar. The perspective of tolerance moves minimally beyond attitudes of *ethnocide* or identity destructiveness that often marginalize or bar groups from receiving full societal benefits. Tolerance often marks an initial step from closed-mindedness toward inclusion.

Xenophobia. The fear or hatred of foreigners or strangers. An expressed dislike of people from other countries, xenophobia embodies discriminatory attitudes and behavior often culminating in violent exhibition of hatred. Synonymous with xenophobia are expressions of racism, ethnocentrism, nationalism, and bigotry. For more information, please see these sites:

- https://www.independent.co.uk/news/science/brexit-prejudice -scientists-link-foreigners-immigrants-racism-xenophobia-leave -eu-a8078586.html
- https://www.washingtonpost.com/news/opinions/wp/2018/10 /23/trump-plays-the-xenophobia-card-again/?noredirect=on& utm_term=.efd888b005f3

Try This Expanding Your Common Language

Now that you have explored our proposed definitions of terms, you can enhance shared understanding and communication. Use the following reflection questions to help you think about the definitions. Once you have completed your personal reflection, share your reflections with a trusted friend, colleague, or family member.

- What definitions align with your thinking and experiences?
- What definitions are you curious to explore in more depth? Why?
- Which definitions are in conflict with how you use the terms?

Try This Talking Across and About Differences

Christine Sleeter, professor emeritus from California State University–Monterey, dedicated much of her career to assisting educators with untying the knots of racism that are woven into the educational system in the United States. Her significant contribution centers around states of mind and the use of language when conversing with people who have different perspectives. Her list of ground rules for discussion is beneficial for fostering productive relationships. Study the list that follows and consider which items you'd like to give the most attention.

As you study the following statements (Sleeter, 2005), consider items that are in most immediate need of your attention. Use the following process.

1. Read the statements and identify the one that you want to focus your attention on, or the one that you want to keep in mind as you communicate with others.

- Keep in mind that differences in perspective are not the problem; the problem is our great difficulty in talking across those differences. Also keep in mind that consensus may not be the goal of discussion. Rather, the main goal may be to understand other points of view. In other words, you should seek understanding, not necessarily agreement.

- It is OK, and often helpful, to speak from your own personal experience. At the same time, recognize that you can't make generalizations from your experience. Your experience is true for you; it may or may not be true for other people.
- When listening to someone speak from her or his experience, listen and do not deny the validity of that experience. You can ask questions for clarification. But watch for conversation stoppers, such as
  — "Yes, but…"
  — "You must have been misinterpreting what happened," and
  — "You shouldn't feel like that."
- Don't interrupt. Wait for the other person to finish and make sure you have actually heard and understood what the other person said before jumping in with what you have to say.
- If you aren't sure you understood what the other person was saying, try paraphrasing what you heard and ask if that is what the person meant. Don't simply dismiss or ignore what the other person said.
- Express disagreement with someone else in a way that acknowledges and respects the point of view that person has articulated. For example, you might say, "I think I see what you are saying. I see the issue differently, though, and here is why."
- If you feel attacked or threatened by what another person is saying, it's OK to express your feelings, but own them. You can say, "I am feeling X about what you just said," but do not attack the other person with statements like "You are being really biased!" You might also take a short time-out before saying anything.
- You don't have to disclose anything you do not wish to disclose. If you are feeling threatened or uneasy and would rather keep your thoughts private, you have a right to do so. Recognize, however, that if we never disclose anything controversial, there would be even less understanding of differences than there is now.

2. After you have identified the statement that you want to focus on, underline key words or phrases that are important to you within that statement.

3. Share your selection with a trusted friend, colleague, or family member. Make sure to share *why* you chose that statement, word, or phrase.

3

Energize with Circular Work

Most "things" in organizations are actually relationships, variables
tied together in a systematic fashion. Events, therefore, depend on
the strength of these ties, the direction of influence, the time it takes
for information in the form of differences to move around circuits.

–Karl Weick (1979, p. 88)

Most of the conversations in schools are organized around the early
20th century industrial structure that was used to mass-produce prod-
ucts. The assembly line structure not only dominated factory work,
but it also affected how cities were organized, how neighborhoods
were constructed, and how schools were put together. We refer to this
arrangement of our physical world and environment as a triangular
world.

As a result of our triangular world, most of our schools still operate in a hierarchical, top-down environment. Note that the triangular
environment uses language that reinforces its structure and helps to

maintain the dominance of the people or positions at the top of the triangle. In fact, if you are unsure about the presence of the triangular structure in your environment, pay close attention to the language people use. In a triangular environment, you will hear the following words and phrases: *top administration, middle management, bottom level, empowerment, the best and the brightest, lower-level learner, average learner, stanine score, fill them with knowledge, mandated, decision input, hold accountable, sanctioned, external design, delivery, external measurement of goal attainment, not enough time, grade levels, advocacy, number one.* We are certain that you can generate a longer list.

The work that we propose features a circular structure highlighted by discovery learning toward a goal of equitable education. It emanates from your moral foundation, which powers all purposeful action. Dialogue operates through slow, unwinding processes that value time differently than most processes that operate in triangular structures. What is effective and efficient in a circular structure may be measured in weeks, years, or even generations. Circular language is innovative and investigative, driven by curiosity. If you are unsure whether you dwell in an environment with circular construction, pay close attention to language around you. In a circular environment, you will hear the following words and phrases: *team, inclusion, voice, colleague, diffuse power, collaboration, consensus, responsibility, create, generate, experiment, internal motivation, time available, each child is gifted, each child learns, each teacher is capable of teaching each student.*

To have circular conversations, you'll need to fully acknowledge your current context and understand the implications the context has on your ability to have meaningful conversations.

People exist in a social organization and organizations are comprised of relationships (Northouse, 2019; Wheatley, 2009). Viewing schools, families, and communities as a woven tapestry of relationships gives us the freedom to see people more holistically. People do not compose household units that are artificially connected to schools through special programs. Individual people are participants in schools and are essential to the health of the school community.

Difficult conversations are critical for improving and fortifying relationships. Martin Luther King Jr. warned of not actively participating in bringing about equitable societal change. When speaking about letting time heal the nation during the civil rights movement, he correctly cited the misfortunes of nonaction by well-intended people who stayed on the sidelines until societal ills got better on their own over time. A masterful southern black preacher and great orator, King stated, "And it may well be that we will have to repent in this generation. Not merely for the vitriolic words of the violent actions of the bad people, but for the appalling silence of indifference of the good people who sit around and say, 'wait on time'" (Carson & Holloran, 2000, p. 209). King's cautionary observation was in 1968. And, to his word, it seems that time remains neutral, siding with no one.

In the United States, Barack Obama was the country's first African American president and he brought hope and a sense of collective relief to many people. "Yes we can" gracefully acknowledged the history of the United States and represented a move from segregationist traditions to help us become a better society. Through the election of an African American to the highest public service office, we chose to see fruition in the work and dreams of many of our ancestors. We thought of Harriet Tubman and her extraordinary work on and achievement with the Underground Railroad. We thought of Crispus Attucks, an African American among the first men to stand for freedom who was gunned down in the Boston Massacre. We also think of women and Latinos—a few have run for but none yet elected to the highest offices. We have experienced the shift from the Stonewall riots to an openly gay candidate entering the race for the White House. It has taken the efforts of many and hundreds of years to move the vision of governing the United States to truly include all citizens. The landscape changes quickly, however, when we choose to be silent. In the 2016 election, for example, 1.7 million people in 33 states and the District of Columbia cast a ballot without voting for the presidential slot (*Washington Post,* December 14, 2016). If those voters had made their selection for the highest office, we don't know how that would have affected the outcome.

Huge societal changes do not happen overnight; however, what we do and where we live and work makes a difference. Small changes over time can influence huge events. In the fast-paced, top-down, triangular world in which many schools operate, we tend to focus on getting things done quickly. We allow relationships to suffer. Time allotments rule our day: 10-minute parent conferences, 60-minute staff meetings, 30-minute lunch periods. Although timelines and some urgency are necessary to achieve outcomes and meet deadlines and goals, we miss opportunities to build meaningful relationships using dialogic circular work. Through continual practice, dialogue builds stronger, healthier relationships among people. When we slow down and get to know one another, we get more accomplished because dialogue fosters better communication and deeper levels of trust. Conversations have the power to create something new and positive in the world (Block, 2008).

In Figure 3.1, note that the triangle is the outer shell and represents the typical configuration of schools, which also protects the hierarchy. The triangle forms borders and sets the framework for the actions that happen within the organization. The borders define the entry and exit of the members. Nestled within the triangle is a circle, representing the process and language that is achieved by discovery conversation through dialogic processes.

Figure 3.1 **Circular Work in a Triangular World**

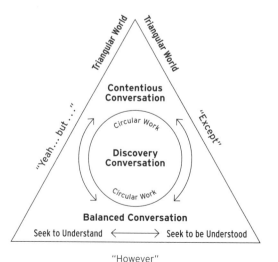

Contentious Conversation. The triangle represents the top-down world in which schools as well as many organizations function. At the top of the triangle is contentious conversation, an experience and place familiar to most of us. Why? We want to be heard. We argue and make our point until we are exhausted or win. Making points represents complete advocacy and helps identify our stance on issues. Usually the interchange of a contentious conversation is rapid. Participants hold on to a predetermined position and strategically engage one another. The main purpose is winning. Each person listens just enough to formulate a rebuttal. In hierarchical organizations in which agendas and executive actions forecast positions and are used to overwhelm opposing ideas, making points or winning is the goal. There are winners and losers where a power dynamic is established and the winner holds supreme control of the relationship.

If someone says, "Let's collaborate," and hands you an agenda, it is not a collaboration. The predetermined agenda establishes the triangular context. As mentioned before, bell schedules and time limits keep us moving and on track—there are specific times and places for making our points, arguing, and debating. The assembly line keeps moving! There is a time and place for advocacy. The important thing to remember is knowing the outcome you want to achieve.

Masked Conversation. The sides of the triangle are held up by some strong dysfunctional supports. When engaging in conversation, language such as *however* and *but* leads the dialogue into an area of masked conversation, otherwise referred to as hiding in plain view. Hiding in plain view means to be physically present and engaged in a conversation without revealing your true perspective on any given issue or topic. Generally, most people retreat to masked conversations around issues they find difficult, like sexual orientation, race, culture, or class. They hide their positions in an attempt to be polite, but this is a practice in deception and is unfortunately prevalent in most schools. When we don't speak from the *cor*, burying feelings and emotions becomes normal and we simply don't show up.

Masked conversations uphold false relationships because the real persons never show up. They hide behind *but, except, however, yeah but,* and use lead phrases such as "I really like what you had to say but..."

or "Your insights are excellent, however…". To understand what is being communicated in a masked conversation, listen to everything after the *but*. It is common for school staff to spend an hour or more in a meeting that is followed by a rush to the parking lot to have the *real* meeting. Avoid masked conversations if you are committed to mindful conversations that move beyond race, class, and culture. Show up. Do not hide in plain view.

Discovery Conversation. Organizations can be complex. Yet complexity is made up of a compilation of simplicities. Discovering the simple things that make things work around you leads to complex changes over time. Although you may be entangled in complex relationships, the practice of dialogic language and processes can lead to discoveries that lower walls and open silos within the triangular structure. In schools, daily routines involve meeting program goals, objectives, test scores, and targets. The stress is high. Dialogue slows processing and infuses renewed energy into lives and relationships. It invites inquiry and unleashes curiosity, a natural motivational igniter for learning. The heart of discovery is the desire to know something other than what is already known, even if what is discovered is known by someone else. Our inability to acknowledge ignorance is a major restraint for discovery conversation. Admitting what I don't know gives the opportunity to unmask myself and learn. It happens in an arena where mistakes are welcomed and forgiveness is practiced. We refer to it as a place of grace, where things are allowed to emerge, where people are not judged for revealing who they are and what they are about. Relationships are built and maintained by knowing yourself and sharing it with others. Discovery conversation requires this perspective.

Balanced Conversation. Balanced conversations involve a balance between contentious conversation—seeking solely to be understood or to win—and discovery conversation—seeking to understand. Balancing ensures efficient and effective decisions. People who are good at balanced conversations move effectively between making points and dialogic inquiry. Proper debate allows several viewpoints to be stated, while dialogue helps everyone understand differing viewpoints. If we only engage in contentious conversations, we will have plenty of action with little to no understanding. By the same token, if all communication happened dialogically, understanding would skyrocket followed by little to no action. Again, knowing the outcome of the conversation is important when deciding which mode of conversation to use. Balanced, discovery, and contentious conversations are all beneficial when used properly.

Conversation Modes: Illustrative Scenarios

To create meaningful relationships, we advocate eliminating masked conversation in relationships. Exchanges in the following scenarios illustrate features of the four conversational modes. Each scenario draws attention to the intent of engagement and the potential corresponding result. The situation begins with the two people fully engaged in contentious conversation.

Scenario 1

Jonas: I am a teacher. I am willing to keep my credential current through professional reading and university coursework. I am willing to come to class prepared. The problem is that those students have parents who don't care enough to make sure their kids come to school to learn.

Juaquin: You have to realize that most parents are doing the best they can. Many of them work two or three jobs and don't have the education to help their children. In my view, they do care about their children and expect you to educate them to high standards.

Jonas: I didn't become an educator to become a social worker! My responsibilities are very clear—to teach! Those who come to school ready to learn receive a great education in my classroom.

Juaquin: Well, it seems to me that you have a very narrow view of our work, and that you are unwilling to entertain any reasonable suggestion. Teaching involves teaching the whole child, not just the part you want to teach.

That conversation is clearly a point-counterpoint interaction. Positions are advocated and held until a winner is declared or one party relents. Let's see if masked conversation has any promise for Jonas and Juaquin.

Scenario 2

Jonas: I am a teacher. I am willing to keep my credential current through professional reading and university coursework. I am willing to come to class prepared. My question is Why don't parents care enough to make sure their kids come to school to learn?

Juaquin: I agree with you, except some parents are barely making it with one job.

Jonas: My parents worked two jobs and they still made it to conferences.

Juaquin: I understand your concerns, but things are different today.

Jonas: Yeah, but working doesn't mean that you don't prepare your kids for learning.

Juaquin: Yeah, kids need to be prepared, but don't you think that is our job too?

Jonas: I see your point, but I can't be a social worker too!

What do you think is going on at this point in the conversation? Have you ever had a similar conversation where you practiced hiding in plain view behind the buts and excepts? Your attempt to appear polite or politically correct simply hid your true thoughts and feelings on the topic. You pretended to agree with the other person while stealthily attacking him or her.

Unlike scenario 2, the following discovery conversation moves through dialogic processes and engagement. It acknowledges a reciprocal power dynamic in which participants view themselves as equals and, by extension, as cocreators of the environment in which they operate. Inquiry is welcomed and questioning a basic premise is highly valued. Clarity becomes essential!

Scenario 3

Jonas: I am a teacher. I am willing to keep my credential current through professional reading and university coursework. I am willing to come to class prepared. My question is, Why don't parents care enough to make sure their kids come to school prepared to learn?

Juaquin: It sounds like "care" is a value of yours. What do you mean by "care"?

Jonas: Yes, I value caring. It means nurturing and doing what needs to be done to ensure success.

Juaquin: Why does that mean so much to you?

Jonas: Well... my parents. They taught me to value caring. They both worked two jobs so I could become a teacher.

Juaquin: It also sounds like you value hard work. Why does that mean so much to you? How does the value of caring square with what you believe about teaching?

Jonas: Teachers should do what they need to do so kids are successful.

Juaquin: So, teachers should work hard and care about their students?

Jonas: Yes, of course.

Juaquin: I believe the same thing. I learned those values from my parents too. I think our students' parents care about their children. Maybe those values look different in different cultures and circumstances. Like you, caring means doing everything I can, so the students are successful. I can't control our students' circumstances, only my response to our students.

Jonas: Hmmmm! I never looked at it that way before. This is really powerful.

Reflect upon the following questions before reading the final scenario.

1. What do Jonas and Juaquin do to encourage balanced dialogue in the last scenario?

2. Do Jonas and Juaquin balance their conversation by seeking to understand each other's perspective?

3. How do they openly reveal their own position on a topic and seek to understand the other's viewpoint through active questioning?

4. Are they aware of their own assumptions and beliefs, and do they know how to express them?

Scenario 4

Jonas: I am a teacher. I am willing to keep my credential current through professional reading and university coursework. I am willing to come to class prepared. My question is, Why don't parents care enough to make sure their kids come to school to learn?

Juaquin: Their parents do care. They are sending the best children they have. They aren't keeping the best ones at home. What assumptions are you making, Jonas?

Jonas: I assume the parents don't care if their child comes to class without doing homework and if they just sit in class and don't do their work.

Juaquin: How might we confirm or dismiss the assumptions we hold about our students' parents?

Jonas: I guess we could hold focus groups to get more information about them. That may help.

Juaquin: That's a great idea. We could also hold some focus groups with our students. In what ways might we explore the values we hold for our students and parents?

Jonas: I have several ideas. Let's get together after school tomorrow and discuss how to make this happen.

Both Juaquin and Jonas experience the opportunity to understand each other's perspective. They seek to understand the feelings and reactions expressed in the exchange. They can have a substantive, enlightening, and effective conversation where they may discover what personally and professionally sustains them as teachers. Their conversation might allow them to better connect with their students and discover that children learn when they are given the right conditions for continuing growth. And, they may come to realize that parents are the biggest supporters of their children's education. Moreover, they may be able to understand that parents send the very best child they have to school and do not lock the good ones at home, away from the classroom. Interrogating their assumptions about parenting leads to a healthier relationship with students.

Free-flowing, open communication provides the lifeblood of a healthy organization. How well we communicate with students, parents, and one another is essential for creating and sustaining strong relationships among people with diverse perspectives and diverse life experiences. Like any skill, mastery of mindful conversation requires practice. Intentional practice with colleagues, friends, and family can help you adapt to different conversation modes. The following activity is designed for use as a professional development exercise, team meeting, department meeting, or family meeting. The intent is to gain perspective as to the various levels of depth experienced in dialogue.

Listen, Hear, and Question

Facilitate the following learning experience, which progresses through rounds and builds upon the information in this chapter. Select four or six willing participants. Seat them in pairs facing their partners at a comfortable distance (about six inches) apart. Attending to the time allowances for each round is critical to the depth of learning.

Round 1. Instruct participants to talk to their partners about anything they want. Limit the conversation to three minutes. Provide no additional guidelines for this round. The objective is for them to experience how they typically talk with one another. It also gives you the opportunity to note how they engage. Observe and note word selection, tone of voice, and the rhythm of the interaction. For example, a courteous exchange of comments might indicate that the participants are engaged in masked conversation. A fast rhythm with few or no questions asked may indicate a contentious conversation is in progress. And a battery of investigative questions and paraphrasing to seek deeper meaning may hint at the presence of discovery conversation.

Round 2. Use strict rules to guide the flow of conversation. It is extremely important that the rules are strictly followed. Unlike the previous conversation, the facilitator chooses the topic. The topic is general enough to allow the person talking to draw from a wide range of experiences and not be rooted in debate (no politics!). The topic of *change* usually works well as a starter. *Change* affects everyone, both personally and professionally. Note that topics that may seem difficult now become rich areas to investigate and harvest using deep learning once dialogic conversation is mastered.

Use the following steps to maximize the learning environment for participants. Tell the pairs to select who will speak first on the topic of *change*.

1. Allow 90 seconds. The person selected is the only one who talks while the partner listens. The listening partner sits stoically and may

not offer head nodding, hand movements, smiles, frowns, or any indicator of agreement or disagreement with the speaking partner. Remind them of the topic, *change*. Give the signal to begin and set the timer. As facilitator, observe. Notice how some participants engage with ease and others struggle. Encourage anyone having trouble to keep talking until you call time.

2. At 90 seconds, use the timer to signal the end. Notice participant response. Most common are sighs of relief, laughter, and comments, such as "that was tough." Do not take questions or ask any. Proceed to the next step.

3. Tell participants to switch roles. The topic is the same, *change*. Use the same rules of engagement for 90 seconds.

4. When the timer signals, ask participants to stop. There will be more laughter and comments. Give participants a moment or two to settle down.

5. Debrief the experience beginning with the question, What was that experience like for you? Responses will likely include that the activity was difficult, they hated it, they found it hard to refrain from smiling or moving, and it didn't feel normal. Some may say they did better as a listener or vice versa. Keep in mind that many will find it difficult to overcome habits such as jumping into conversations without fully listening to their partner. Some may admit being startled by what they have come to know about themselves.

Complete the debriefing by sharing your reason for the restraints. Explain that because the listeners were held back from using normal behaviors, they would experience tension from avoiding their cultural tendencies of expression as well as notice what verbal and nonverbal signals they needed to squelch. Reinforce the idea that culture in its most simple form consists of values and beliefs that people agree are normal expressions (Schein, 2004). Hand gesturing, head nodding in agreement or head shaking in disagreement, smiling—each behavior expresses values manifested through agreed-upon standard behaviors. Providing an alternative perspective (staying silent and avoiding signals) accentuates the point that there are different normative behaviors. Emphasize that all cultures express values but use these verbal and nonverbal behaviors differently. For example, many indigenous

First Nations people find it offensive to smile or make eye contact with a speaker. They believe these behaviors are rude and draw attention away from the speaking party—and that they also refocus attention on the listener. Asking participants to restrain from outward expression creates tension, helps most of us experience our own assumptions, and makes the right or wrong way of behaving visible and apparent to others. While restrained, typically, participants come to realize their cultural normative tendencies, causing it to bubble up from beneath the surface, making it a known quality. A good rule of measure is the understanding that when your cultural surrounding serves you well, you are unaware of its existence. The more conscious you are of the values and beliefs that guide your behavior, the more fluidly you will move through dialogic conversation.

Round 3. Participants begin a structured process to learn and practice conversational skills. *Do not tell the participants how much time they have to talk.* (Allow a minimum of 8 minutes.)

1. Prepare participants to have a free-flowing conversation with their partner using the stems of what, why, where, when, and who. In this round, each pair can choose the "what" or topic to discuss. Choosing the topic fuels motivation and is an agreed-upon starting point to ignite curiosity. In a free-flowing conversation, encourage participants to ask at least three "why" questions to uncover assumptions and predispositions around the topic. For example, a participant discovers an association with control when the topic is *change.* Questions might be *Why is it necessary to be in control of change? Why is control important? Why do we feel out of control at times?* The questions seek to help the listener understand the speaker's perspective and also helps the speaker understand her/his perspective and stance and to understand the foundation of the perspective of both parties. Ask an additional three to five "why" questions. Note that the party receiving questions is not treated suspiciously and that the questions may be answered by either party, allowing for reciprocal clarification. The idea is to uncover predispositions about the subject and free the values, beliefs, and assumptions that are underneath it. If participants express discomfort with asking questions ("why"), remind them that 2-year-old

children are masters of that question as they pursue knowledge—asking *why* is the mindset they need to begin the journey.

2. Encourage participants to ask *where* and *when* questions. *Where* and *when* questions help with contextualization using time and location. To extend the questioning strategies mentioned earlier, *Where did you learn that change was good or bad? When in your life did you develop such attitudes? Where (or when) did you get the notion that change is controllable?* Answers to questions of this kind open the conversation to discovery and allow revelations of self and others to fill the void.

3. Finally, encourage the participants to ask "who?" to help identify the relationships associated with values or assumptions that guide actions. Understanding "when," "where," and "from whom" values and beliefs were taught becomes a powerful window into knowing what supports and justifies seemingly logical action. Consider questions such as the following: *From whom did you learn that change was controllable? Who taught you to value change in the way you do?* It has been our experience that participants, upon discovering *why, where, when,* and *who* connections, realize that many of their values and behaviors function as unspoken contracts made with people important in their early development. The realization alone provides opportunity to question, retain, modify, or replace values or beliefs—the ultimate compass points for actions.

4. Invite participants to have a conversation using the *why, where, when, who* stems. Tell them they can respond nonverbally by nodding their heads, smiling, or moving their hands. Do not tell them the amount of time allotted, but allow 8–10 minutes.

5. When time is called, debrief with the following prompts:
- What was *that* experience like for you? Typical responses include it was great, more in-depth, fun, felt natural.
- How does this dialogue compare with the conversations that take place in your work or home setting?

Announce that they were allotted up to 10 minutes for the unrestricted conversation. Participants usually remark that time felt longer during the allotted 90 seconds with restricted engagement versus the 8–10 minutes of unrestricted engagement. The conclusion often cited is that free expression of cultural norms nurtures the easy exchange of ideas, fostering accelerated learning and engagement.

Participants frequently express surprise at the high volume of their inner voice exposed in round 2, which wants to assert itself and interrupt what their partner is saying. For many, it is the first time they are made aware of the inner struggle to actually quiet themselves and listen to someone else. The natural tendency is to jump in and advocate a point rather than seek to understand the alternative perspective. Participants note that the questioning strategies guided by the stems of what, why, when, where, and who help to suspend their tendencies to advocate for themselves and their point of view and sets the stage for a deep exploratory dive. They also become conscious of the fun they had taking a deep dive into a shared investigation of expanding their horizons.

4

Coconstruct
Brave Spaces

In preceding chapters, we discussed communication as essential to building and maintaining relationships. Aware of the power of person-to-person communication, we understand that building effective relationships involves understanding the *whys* of individual and group behaviors. Once the *why* is clear—the moral imperative for each of us—the *what* and *how* become attainable. When you practice effective communication, there is a high likelihood that the requisite skills and attitudes will carry over into informal conversations with your colleagues, friends, and family. You'll begin to see that conversation is an important component in developing your capacity to have conversations that go beyond race, class, and culture.

In her powerful book *Turning to One Another,* Margaret Wheatley (2009) tells us that conversation is an ancient art form that comes naturally to people. She warns that people are becoming increasingly isolated and fragmented, however, and need one another more than ever. We agree with her as we consider the environment in most schools.

Schools are where adults spend more than eight hours a day interacting with students without having many effective conversations with other adults. Formal meetings and professional development sessions are frequently one-way, top-down information distribution exercises. Regimented circumstances give little opportunity to nurture the deep, substantive conversations that bind relationships. Bell schedules and other rigid time structures effectively weaken connections and fracture groups, leaving adults to communicate haphazardly in hallways, faculty lounges, or parking lots (Wenger & Snyder, 2000).

Settings where adults sneak in a few passing words are poor places for holding critical conversations. The autopilot questions such as "How was your weekend?" and "how are you doing?" are usually met with casual responses of "Fine" or "We're doing well." Although these questions are considered to be a manifestation of good manners, they serve as conversation enders. They send clear signals to other people that they should stay in their lane. Yet, our classrooms and schools need to foster conditions that encourage participation in critical conversations. We need conditions that invite free movement among and throughout perceived lanes of separation to build and strengthen relationships that factor into the education (intended or not) of our students.

Designing and maintaining conditions that foster meaningful conversations are essential for advancing and maintaining strong relationships. Some conversation processes promote free and open communication; others obstruct the exchange of ideas and experiences and lead to miscommunication. Relationships require understanding and mastering communication skills and safe and brave spaces in which communication can occur.

Safe and Brave Spaces

Although speaking honestly is essential to meaningful conversation, we do run the risk of offending other people. Most people avoid critical conversations if they anticipate that emotions may become volatile. For instance, we facilitated a workshop in which a white teacher referred to her African American students as "precious little monkeys."

She intended the term affectionately and saw nothing wrong with her phrasing. When she made the remark, however, we saw an earthquake of shudders from participants of color. Yet, not a word was spoken by any of the participants. A heavy atmosphere and a deafening silence filled the room. We called for the morning break during which several people asked us, as facilitators, what were we going to do about the comment. Our response to each of them was "How are *you* going to handle the situation?" It was obvious to them and to us that the teacher had unknowingly and unintentionally offended several people. Emotions were high and it was obvious we could not continue with the planned agenda. It was clear to us that the participants were avoiding the situation and wanted someone else to handle it. We firmly suggested to the teachers who brought this problem to our attention that they needed to have a dialogue with the person. It was time for them to use the skills they were learning to have a critical conversation. With a little encouragement from us, they agreed. We asked the participant who had made the comment if she would participate in a dialogue. She cautiously agreed.

A little perspective is needed—this group had been together for a year and this was their sixth of eight sessions together. Yet, safety was critical and we needed to be sure that every participant felt safe enough to have the conversation. We gathered the whole group in a large circle, placing the dialogue volunteers in the center. The following script captures what happened.

Facilitator: Just before the break, a comment was made that requires us to have a critical conversation. The comment was not intended to offend. When Marie referred to her students as "my precious little monkeys," several people felt offended. Lawrence, Faith, and Marie have agreed to have a dialogue regarding the situation.

Faith: I know you care about your students, Marie. I have worked with you for 10 years and hold you in high regard. That is not my concern. My concern is that you used a term, *monkeys*, that culturally has been used as a derogatory term for African Americans. When I was in school, the teacher actually referred to us, her African American students, as monkeys and sat us together on one side of the room, separated from the other students. How have you experienced the term *monkey*?

Marie: I could tell you were upset but I couldn't figure out why. I was afraid to ask because I didn't want to cause any conflict. When I was a child, my daddy used to call me Monkey. It was a term of endearment. As a matter of fact, I was watching *Hawaii Five-O* the other night and the character, Danny Williams, lovingly called his little girl Monkey. It brought back such fond memories of me and my dad. I had no idea I was offending you when I referred to my students as such.

Lawrence: Wow, I have learned a lot in these few minutes. I was so upset during the break that I could hardly talk. I assumed that you were being racist and insensitive. But after listening to you, I can see the situation differently. I am sorry to have thought of you in those terms.

Marie: I am too. I had no idea that the term had a derogatory meaning for African Americans. I am also learning so much. I offer apologies for my ignorance. As a teacher, it is my responsibility to know as much as possible to ensure the trust of my children. How many students have I offended over the years because of what I bring with me? Thank you for this insight. Because of it, I will do better.

Facilitator: I know this was scary for the three of you. You all did an amazing job using the skills you have learned. The confidence you displayed was admirable. Because you summoned the courage to have this conversation, you were able to come to a shared understanding around such a simple but racially charged word. Keep reminding yourselves that behaviors that are offensive to you may not be personal; they may be cultural. Many of our conflicts can be solved or at least understood through dialogues where we seek to understand one another and develop a collective vision beyond cultural boundaries.

This scenario demonstrates a situation in which participants took off the armor of deceit and deflection that is often used to protect us from being attacked. Because they were in a safe space and had worked to gain trust as a group, they were free to speak from the *cor*. They acknowledged what they didn't know, opening the opportunity to learn from each other. Perceived cultural boundaries were crossed and learning took place. In the final analysis, their horizon—their field of vision—expanded, allowing them to add to their cultural understanding and knowledge, not lose, as is often assumed.

Krownapple (2017) contends that brave and safe spaces are necessary components to critical conversations. The term "safe space" has been used to indicate comfortable or risk-free environments. Krownapple posits that brave space "acknowledges the unavoidable risk, struggle, and discomfort that accompany authentic engagement" (p. 48). We support both notions—that we need to create structures and an environment that fosters taking unavoidable risks that support critical conversations. Safety and risk are not mutually exclusive. Although we created a safe environment and used the structure of a circle for Lawrence, Faith, and Marie during the workshop, their encounter was not risk-free. They each took a risk by engaging in the conversation. No one knew how it would go or where it would end. However, it was clear to us, as facilitators, that no gain would be achieved without engagement.

Yet, the greater illusion is in the belief that there is space between us, when in fact we are all connected. Our goal through conversation is to reveal our interconnectedness so that our relationships can move beyond the physical limitations that are perceived, such as race, class, culture, sexual orientation, and religion. It is not that we do not see those things *about* one another but that we see ourselves *in* one another. The power that Lawrence, Marie, and Faith used to reach beyond their preconceived notions was already within them. They moved beyond negative motivators of fear, anger, or guilt and summoned the courage to have a conversation that led to a deeper shared meaning that embraced each of them. Thus, they discovered their interconnectedness. They now move through the world aware of their connection—not their physical disconnection resulting from different early familial influences. Initially, brave and safe spaces are important, but not nearly as vital as discovering the safe and brave states of mind that already exist within you.

Much of the hesitation around joining critical conversations to advance equity is grounded in an ego investment associated with potential perceived attacks, particularly as it relates to advantage. Some people may shy from conversations intended to advance the social and intellectual benefit of children of color because they perceive the potential of losing personal and societal group identity advantage. This is not a small point, as the majority of children in U.S. schools are of color and are taught primarily by white teachers. As a group, educators have historically benefitted from a racially constructed system that is administered to their advantage. As discussed earlier, such advantages are often normed as "the way it is" using the argument that "those children" need to get with the program, work hard, and learn. Asking white teachers to actively give up this advantage to children considered to be socially or innately disadvantaged becomes the heart of the equity work. Acknowledging schools and households as gathering places of closely interconnected human relationships is a step toward acknowledging that every child is gifted and talented. It is our job, as educators, to nurture their talents and help children learn to believe in themselves.

With Whom Do I Start?

The quick and easy answer is to begin with you. The slow and hard answer is to begin with you. Knowing who you are and what you value is crucial to beginning the journey of getting to know yourself better. You have probably heard the saying "anything worth having is worth doing." In our experience, critical conversations are worth having and doing. The hard work demands that we question deeply held values, assumptions, and beliefs. As you critique what you value and believe, it becomes clear how they link to your actions. You may discover that some deeply held values, assumptions, and actions no longer serve you well. You may be valuing, assuming, believing, or behaving the way you do only because you have always unquestionably done so (Schein, 2004). A story best illustrates how following unquestioned beliefs can distort purpose.

> A young girl watched with great attention as her mother prepared a ham for the traditional holiday dinner. She watched her mother use a sharp carving knife to cut away both ends of the ham and place it into the roasting pan. Curious, she questioned her mother's technique.

"Why do you need to cut off the ends of the ham?"

"Because that's how my mother taught me," the mother replied.

"Will it make the ham taste better?"

"Well, it's your grandmother's recipe. It doesn't get any better than that!" the mother responded fondly.

Her curiosity still roaring, the young girl asked her grandmother about why the ham was cut at both ends before being placed in the pan.

"It's the way my mother taught me," came the reassuring response from her grandmother. Still unsatisfied, the girl decided to seek one more source, her great-grandmother. Surely, she would give the definitive answer. When asked, her great-grandmother replied, "Well, dear, I had to cut the ends off the ham because I didn't have a big enough pan for it."

This amusing story makes the point that much of what we do can be traced to generational norms once deemed *right* for the circumstance in which they were used. However, what was considered right in a past generation has a good chance of being *wrong* in the current one. Unless the question of why is raised, we are doomed to participate in unnecessary, wasteful, and sometimes hurtful traditions.

Doing the work of interrogating traditions requires a childlike curiosity and a willingness to dig beneath the surface. Values, beliefs, and assumptions are usually steeped in traditions, and unveiling them can be hard work. More difficult is to cross-examine what we do and answer the question "Do these still serve me well?" Self-examination fosters productive, meaningful cross-cultural conversations that can foster and strengthen relationships.

In a 1960s sermon called "A Knock at Midnight" (cassette recording, 1998), Dr. Martin Luther King Jr. suggests that humankind has advanced technologically to conquer outer space, but humankind has not had the moral commitment to conquer their inner space. We concur with King and offer that the quest to conquer our inner space is a work in progress. It develops from regions deep underneath the intellectual veneer that is small talk and masked conversation. Conquering inner space demands willful and purposeful change that exceeds simple cognition or intellectual knowledge about a transformation of self.

As you reflect upon safe and brave spaces, think of your inner space. The condition of your inner space is of utmost importance. We do not view space as distance in the traditional sense, but more of an attitude. Consider the following acrostic (SPACE):

State of mind: Am I open or closed to what the other person has to offer? Am I willing to give what I have to another? What is my intent in this relationship? What drives me? Am I positively motivated by friendliness, exploration, or stewardship? Or, am I motivated by assertiveness, competition, or craving?

Practice forgiveness (self and others): Am I capable of letting go of the breaches in trust experienced in previous relationships? Can I stand in the present and let go of the past? Do I experience the present, or do I move through the world looking backward and missing what's in front of me?

Acknowledge disappointments: Am I able to acknowledge disappointments that result from broken promises and breaches in expected outcomes? Do I see how I might have caused fissures in relationships?

Courage: Am I aware of my *cor*? What values operate in what I believe about the world? What beliefs shape my actions? Will I summon my *cor* to do what is right or stick with what may be considered legal regardless of whether it is truly right?

Engage willfully: Am I willing to be influenced by others as much as I want others to be influenced by me? Do I see myself in another person?

You are your greatest asset in all that you do. Getting you *right* is key for successful participation in critical conversations. Otherwise, you will likely return to dependable defensive tactics of combative conversations, masking conversations, or avoiding conversations entirely.

Fierce Conversations

Susan Scott (2004) reminds us that "the conversation is the relationship" (p. 6). She views fierce conversation as essential to sustaining healthy relationships. Scott's notion of "fierce" is less frightening than it might seem at first glance. Participants are encouraged to approach conversations intensely, robustly, untamed, and unbridled. "In its simplest form," she states, "a fierce conversation is one in which we come out from behind ourselves into the conversation and make it real" (p. 7). Unveiling ourselves may sound risky, but it is necessary to authentic conversation. In fact, we argue that unmasking relieves pressure by lessening the amount of energy required to hide in plain view.

Ken Blanchard, in the foreword to Scott's book, presents her seven principles for mastering the fierce conversation. We have taken Blanchard's list and explained the meaning of each principle as it relates to our focus in this book.

Principle 1: Master the courage to interrogate reality. Do not take for granted the way the world has been handed to you. Take on a two-year-old child's mindset and ask the big question, *why*? This simple questioning strategy, which every toddler performs unrelentingly, unearths what is beneath our assumptions about the world.

Principle 2: Come out from behind yourself into the conversation and make it real. Real is *what* you are at the core. *Who* you are is a façade made of the social definers encased within cultural boundaries. How you act, speak, or live can be changed at any moment when or should you decide to do so. Real conversation demands that real people remove their façade.

Principle 3: Be here, prepared to be nowhere else. Be in the conversation. Bring yourself to the exchange and stay until the conversation is finished. Don't take a mental vacation while physically present. The *now* is the only moment we have. All other moments have either happened or may never happen. Now is the only manageable moment.

Principle 4: Tackle your toughest challenge today. What makes a problem a problem is the inability or unwillingness to view what is in front of you in a different way. Letting go of old ideas through conversation with others opens up the possibility of experiencing something new. Conversation becomes the agitator from which ideas spring and innovation occurs.

Principle 5: Obey your instincts. Blanchard's commentary about this principle is priceless. "Don't just trust your instincts—obey them. Your radar works perfectly. It's the operator who is in question" (p. xv). The goal of this book is to focus on the operator rather than the residuals. When you view yourself as a central variable in the human family, the results take care of themselves.

Principle 6: Take responsibility for your emotional wake.
What you say matters. The words you speak can strongly affect others
as they navigate cross-cultural boundaries. Assume positive intentions
and put forth your best authentic self. Take responsibility for what is
shared.

Principle 7: Let silence do the heavy lifting. Invite silence. The
void is a bubble that gives birth to possibility. It is the place of potential.
It is the moment where thinking is valued as contributing, not detract-
ing. Silence pushes away the noise that surrounds our thoughts and
creates opportunity for new ideas.

Coconstructing Meaning

When faced with disparaging or negative comments or questions, your
community members may get stuck. Although walking away from negative comments may feel the easiest solution, that action gives power
and permission to speakers who use hurtful and harmful words. To
avoid giving bullies power, intentionally practice fierce conversations
with friends, colleagues, and family. The big question is, What will you
say?

To respond appropriately, we suggest practicing and becoming
masterful at asking questions of yourself and others. Questions have
the uncanny ability to break patterns and tunnel a path of opportunity.
Being skilled at asking questions about values, beliefs, and assumptions
allows examination of the origins of such, which allows us to ascertain
if those values, beliefs, and assumptions continue to serve us well.
Careful scrutiny can determine which values, beliefs, and assumptions
are root causes of damaging conversations in which we've engaged.
At that crucial revelation, we can make the moral choice to change.
The conversation shifts to a focus of possibility through questions
posed from positive intentionality, inclusive, and exploratory language
(Lindsey et al., 2009; Scott, 2004). When people competently communicate with one another, they are authentically generating and sharing information. Meaning is consensually coconstructed and leads to
coherent bonds within relationships.

In the following scenario, we focus on a conversation between two teachers, Jackie and Asia. They engage in a reflective dialogue about the workshop they recently attended. Asia struggles to understand her deep emotional reactions to the workshop that was focused on questioning values, beliefs, and assumptions. She asked Jackie, a trusted colleague, to help make sense of her feelings. Jackie had sponsored the workshop, and Asia felt safe in sharing her concerns and questions with Jackie.

Asia: Jackie, you know from the very beginning, I have been in full support of you and the efforts we are making to ensure that the language we use describes our students in ways that raises our expectations of them and of ourselves. But, after our workshop yesterday, something is really bothering me.

Jackie: What is it, Asia? How can I help you?

Asia: Well, I guess mostly by just listening.

Jackie: Is it fair to ask "hard, maybe difficult" questions?

Asia: Oh, that's scary. What do you mean?

Jackie: Well, maybe I am anticipating your comments, but I am struck by your using the phrase about "being in full support of you and the efforts." Do you want to begin?

Asia: Well, yeah. I am stunned by how quickly you went to the heart of the matter. Jackie, I listened to the facilitator talk about our moral and ethical responsibility to have critical conversations. I have engaged in the activities and read books on dialogue, but I cannot escape feeling blamed.

Jackie: Describe for me what you mean by "feeling blamed."

Asia: Ay! Sometimes I feel angry, as if I'm being accused of something that I had nothing to do with. Other times I feel guilty for not knowing about these things already. However, I know those feelings are not productive, so I just sit on them.

Jackie: No, you don't, Asia. You internalize them to anger, guilt, or frustration. I am never sure which it is.

Asia: What do you mean?

Jackie: OK, we've been friends and colleagues for several years, and I think I know a little about you as a person. Frankly, Asia, you seem to want us all to change immediately. I think the facilitator has really tried to help us see that the journey to create a more authentic culture isn't just our latest project. It's a process through which we have to challenge our values and beliefs and, hopefully, our interactions with our students. Our values and beliefs are most evident in the assumptions we have about our students.

Asia: I think I understand that. But, what do you mean about my wanting "us to change immediately"? Isn't that what we're supposed to do?

Jackie: Remember what our facilitator said yesterday: We must understand the long-term effects of systems of oppression. For example, think about racism and how it affects people at both a personal and institutional level, not only for the oppressed but the oppressor.

Asia: Yeah. OK.

Jackie: Let me know if this makes sense to you. Racism negatively affects both the victims and perpetrators. Let's take the historical periods of slavery and Jim Crow. African Americans were obviously affected by the loss of personal liberty and being confined, at best, to second-class citizenship. At the same time, the rest of the population, mostly white, lost moral bearing in allowing such practices to persist. Does that make sense?

Asia: Unfortunately, yes, it makes a lot of sense. I don't know what to do with the information and how that affects the here and now of our school and my classroom.

Jackie: Mostly, until we confront legacies of racism, it interjects destructive energy into the system—like the school or a classroom. By understanding the double-edged effects, we are more able to see and feel the effects of oppression on our students and ourselves and work to combat it. We are more prepared to ask ourselves hard questions about our own assumptions and how they affect ourselves and others. It's not easy to question our intentions, especially the intentions that are unwittingly institutionalized in our organizations. And yet, this is the only way we can change things. The facilitator's comment that one of the major impediments to school reform is that those who have benefitted from current practices don't see a need to change. That resonated with me. In other words, the system serves them well, so there must be something wrong with students or cultures that are not served well. Thus, our negative language we use to describe them like *"those* kids" or "students with special needs have parents that don't care."

Asia: Let's suppose you are accurate and, believe me, I am beginning to see the situation in ways you describe them—then why do I feel stuck and blamed?

Jackie: Your feelings are natural and normal. A hard question you might ask is, What are *you* willing to do, and how are *you* willing to change to create the best learning culture for every student at this school? We can't be observers in this change process. We are the leaders. Our feelings can indicate that we are on the verge of deeper and more powerful learning.

Asia: You make my being "stuck" sound like resistance or denial.

Jackie: Just imagine—if you have the feelings you are describing, what it is like for the students who are not succeeding at this school? Think about how your students' parents must feel when they don't see our school as "value added" for their children. They also may feel angry, guilty, and frustrated by the circumstances.

A quick analysis of Asia and Jackie's conversation reveals four of the seven fierce conversation principles at work.

Principle 1: Master the courage to interrogate reality. Asia invited Jackie to interrogate her and that demonstrates courage. It created a space for both to engage in *cor,* strengthening through the inquiry process.

Principle 2: Come out from behind yourself into the conversation and make it real. Making the conflict explicit created the opportunity for interrogating thoughts or experiences that dwelled in their subconsciousness. When raising questions, the possible comes into focus.

Principle 3: Be here, prepared to be nowhere else. Jackie engaged with Asia to deal with her concern. She didn't drift into another space but chose to address Asia's concern. She further suspended her personal thoughts long enough to hear what was being said.

Principle 4: Tackle your toughest challenge today. They dove into the conversation the moment that interest surfaced. There was no "waiting for the right time" to have the critical conversation. They approached the situation with an attitude that "the time is always ripe to do right!" (Carson & Holloran, 1998, p. 210). Treat all time as precious and be prepared to engage at any moment.

Also evident in their dialogue are elements found in the acrostic SPACE. They effectively collapsed perceived separation and approached the conversation with a unified mind:

State of mind: Am I willing to be influenced by another or to give what I have to someone else? There is a clear invitation to gain the perspective of another through a request. Asia's appeal signaled Jackie to see the world through Asia's eyes. Just as important, Jackie accepted the invitation and let the invitee know that "I'm with you."

Practice forgiveness: Can I acknowledge my role and let go of memories of broken relationships? They discussed the emotional trauma associated with receiving unearned benefit through systems of oppression that may be invisible to them. Letting go of negative emotional energy associated with this circumstance becomes the hard work of forgiveness.

Acknowledge disappointments: Do I acknowledge disappointments resulting from broken promises and breaches in expected outcomes? With Jackie's encouragement, Asia acknowledged that parents experience disappointment when teachers are unable to meet their hopes and aspirations for their children.

Courage: What values are operational in the way I believe? Throughout the exchange they freely examine the conundrum through their *cor*—governing values and beliefs. They examined the values and beliefs that were presented in the workshop that caused Asia's discomfort. In the final analysis, they wrestled with how the workshop experience created imbalance in what they value, believe, and how they move through the world.

Engage willfully: Do I have the will to be involved with others and to be influenced by them? Asia's invitation and Jackie's acceptance demonstrates mutual willful engagement. From that point, the problem was no longer viewed through a fractured lens that rendered separate worldviews but through a shared focus.

Asia and Jackie willfully reciprocated scrutiny of moral reference points. Together, they traveled beyond traditional conversational patterns that mask who they are. The perceived boundaries between them vanished, establishing a common problem to reconcile. Together, they exposed crevices in their morality and explored the ethical stances of what they *ought* to do in the attempt to establish what they *will* actually do (Habermas, 1990). Their exchange allows us a glimpse of ourselves when encountering something that might be seen as a problem, such as children who *ought* not be in our schools or people who *ought* not be in our country. When we collapse the distance between us, we create the opportunity to see ourselves in other situations and gain a view of how things might be approached differently. It allows us to be free to disentangle values and beliefs that potentially blind us to reality. Crippling emotional states of fear, anger, and guilt—as well as denial—are cast aside.

Although the elements and ideas within Susan Scott's fierce conversations and SPACE are important, do not dwell on memorizing them or getting them right. Practice a few at a time. Remember the most important components of any conversation are you and other people in the relationship.

Exploring Values

Try This

Exploring our personal values, how we experience those values, and how other people experience us related to our values is an important conversation. Use this activity to examine a value and explore how it shows up in everyday actions—and to consider how it influences how we see others.

1. Ask a trusted friend, family member, or colleague to engage in this experience with you.

2. With your partner, review the example that explores the value of hard work. Then, each of you should choose your own value to explore, reflect on, and share. Remember that a value is something that you appreciate or deem important.

A value that I learned from the family in which I grew up: *Hard Work*

How do I experience this value?
- Arriving early, staying late at my workplace to give projects the attention they deserve.
- Being prepared for meetings.
- Meeting my self-imposed or self-directed deadlines.

How does this value affect the interactions I have with the adults with whom I work?
- I expect people to be as prepared as I am for meetings.
- I negatively judge people who miss a determined deadline.

How do I believe others might experience me, related to this value?
- I work hard by arriving early and staying late because I don't have kids.
- I must be a fast worker despite my processing disorder, which means it takes me longer to complete projects.
- I am trying to "kiss up" to leaders.

3. With your partner, share your values and discuss your reflections.

5

Communicate with the Power of Trust

One of the most important things you do is communicate with someone else. The urgency to sensibly communicate can be heightened when the climate threatens to maintain classism, racism, xenophobia, homophobia, and other anxieties associated with the allocation of social power. Not only must we communicate with one another, but we must do it competently.

Jürgen Habermas (1990) gives insight as to key elements of competent communicating that can lead to what he terms "communicative action." The hallmark of communicative action is two or more people engaging in dialogic conversation with the intent of coming to an agreement about something they encounter in the objective (outside) world. In their discussion, they agree to use subjective (internal) reference points to make sense of external occurrences. The internal references are drawn from what Habermas terms the "lifeworld."

Lifeworld

Imagine your life experiences as a wellspring and you have the ability to draw from it to solve problems, understand situations, and formulate plans of action. This wellspring is what Habermas (1990) calls the lifeworld—the sum of your life experiences that operate as background. The lifeworld undergirds all presuppositions you make—and nestled within are cultural patterns, rules, and regulations that shape your view of the world and establish parameters for your vision and identity. Your gender identity, racial identity, ethnic identity, faith association, and social assignment coalesce within the lifeworld.

The lifeworld provides the information that fills your conversations and your daily life, whether you are aware of its presence. Your idea of reality is made of experiences that are stored in your lifeworld, projected into the objective world. Everyday lifeworld experiences lead to everyday objective realities. For example, your notion of a wooden table is labeled according to how you have experienced it. Beyond a collection of cells that were once a tree, you may experience it as the cultural object that is to be used as a place for dining or propping your digital tablet. Your familiarity with it most likely depends upon how you have come to culturally associate it based upon the experiences you have with other people. Comfortable, pretty, and useful are all descriptors of cultural associations with a wooden table. This example emphasizes that what you call an object (a table) and how you experience it in the objective (outer) world is born from the experiences referenced in your subjective (inner) world. Be conscious of your participation in this phenomenon.

Bring Lifeworld Forward

Because we constantly subconsciously process our lifeworld experiences, how do we purposefully and consciously engage these experiences in our everyday interactions? Good question. Conscious awareness and purposeful use of the lifeworld requires us to let go of egocentric methods that are intended to strategically overpower an opponent, as in raw debate. Adopting an attitude where your primary goal is to reach consensus with someone about what you encounter or observe in the objective world is the pathway for coconstructing an equitable reality. Our expectation is that you intentionally engage and share your lifeworld while you are involved in conversation.

Maintaining positive intention about working toward consensual agreement is fundamental when entering authentic relationships with others who have vastly different lifeworlds. Entering a multicultural space committed to an inclusive community requires negotiating a variety of points of view. The high probability of different lifeworld reference points and data streams converging produces opportunities for rich perspectives. Having positive intent lowers the risk of highly contentious conflict among widely varying perspectives.

Reaching consensual agreement through reciprocal engagement about what is objectively observed happens when each party *describes* what they initially perceive based upon their lifeworld experience. They then negotiate and agree upon a new description or experience. Herein lies the collective work of extending old ways of understanding to creating new ways. Through communicative action, it is possible to move from a *described* world where race matters to an agreed-upon *redescribed* world for which race is an illusion and carries zero value. This redescribed world allows new possibilities.

Conversational Pathways and Claims of Validity

Reaching new understandings in a dialogic format is an important focus of this book. Purposeful engagement among people with different lifeworlds requires you to be responsible for participating in civil discourse. As mentioned previously, the opportunities for multiple conversational mishaps are myriad given multicultural lifeworld experiences. Yet the opportunity for expanding our perspectives and relationships through purposeful conversation is rich.

It is possible for people entwined in the same conversation to travel two separate pathways. One pathway is paved with *strategic action* (contentious conversation or raw debate), while the other features *inquiry* (discovery conversation or dialogue). Parties traveling down the corridor oriented toward strategic action use maneuvers designed to win over the other's perspective. They may even go so far as to sabotage the conversation for the sake of claiming the win. Familiar power tactics (e.g., "I am your boss. So, it's my way or the highway") are common practices. Contentious conversation highlighted with raw debate is the primary method of communicating, with winning the argument as the objective. Another prominent feature of contentious conversations is masked conversation, during which one or more participants appear to agree with something or someone that they do *not* agree with. When taking the strategic action path, a group can arrive at an end point without knowing how they got there or why the journey commenced.

In contrast, the pathway of discovery conversation proceeds through inquiry with the goal of reaching consensual *agreement* about something encountered in the real world, such as equitable schools. Parties engage in honest exploration of the topic openly sharing and questioning each of their lifeworld experiences to form a predicate for a possible new understanding of something they both view as old. Out of this exchange, a shift in perspective emerges. An example of such a shift is when schools forthrightly consider the yearly calendar relative to the change in student demographics of the students they serve. The current educational calendar for most U.S. public schools is based upon traditional norms of the Anglo-Saxon Christian tradition. Restructuring the district calendar so that it is more inclusive of nondominant faith-based groups such as Muslim, Hindi, Buddhist, and Jewish, to name a few, would be more equitable. Many school employees of these groups are frequently penalized by needing to take personal leave or students receive an "excused absence" when the dominant group does not have to do the same. These current practices maintain structural unfairness and systemic injustices.

We wish to highlight that society functions as a collective. How we go about our daily tasks as a collective is dependent upon the way we choose to come together. An assembly oriented toward strategic action in conversation most often leads to dictatorial and egocentric outcomes. An assembly of people with an attitude of discovery through dialogue can achieve heightened understanding. When we learn more about one another and acknowledge that our lifeworlds are linked, we see ourselves as one and the same and make our community stronger.

Validity Claims

How do you know what is being communicated is dependable and valid? Communicative action requires application of conditions that let us know the acceptability of what is said. These are called validity claims (Habermas, 1990). We use three measures to gauge if what is being said is suitable: *truth, rightness,* and *truthfulness.* Although we do not present what individuals consider as truth, rightness, or truthfulness to be a universal objective, we do consider these three subjective claims when establishing what is perceived is judged valid.

These three claims are subjective and operate subconsciously. We use them to determine whether the conversation is open or shut, frank or dishonest, continues or terminates. In the quest for "the truth" or "who is right," be mindful of the subjective nature of truth, right, and truthfulness and how using them to establish legitimacy of what is being said influences the daily coconstruction of our objective world. Recognizing that our world is consensually coconstructed opens the probability for accepting that my truth looks different from your truth. In turn, this puts us in a position to have a conversation that leads to a common truth between us, particularly around the topic of equity. Our intent is to highlight the importance of these three points of measure as legitimate claims for consensual agreement rather than advocating which truth is the "real truth." More important, we contend that everyone becomes comfortable with the relative nature of our objective world and its dependencies upon our taking responsibility for coconstructing it.

Listed below are terms to further describe application of each validity claim. Each term is applied to the worthiness of what is spoken by the other party when considering whether to agree with their perspective. Study the list and consider how you might measure the worthiness of your agreement or disagreement with someone as you converse and interact with them.

Truth: certainty, reality, actuality, veracity, genuine

Rightness: correctness, appropriateness, aptness, exactness, properness

Truthfulness: honesty, openness, candor, frankness, faithfulness

When we engage in conversation, we automatically register a yes or no response when considering what is spoken against the measures of truth, rightness, and truthfulness. Each person ponders if what is being said by the other party is real, appropriate, or honest. All three metrics gauge whether what is being said is valid. A yes response indicates that the conversation is valid and signals it is safe to pursue inquiry toward further understanding. A no response indicates that what was said fails at least one of the tests and the conversation is deemed invalid, halting the pursuit of further understanding.

Trust Matters

Trust is a major force for establishing cohesive relationships and moving conversations across borders of perceived social-political, cultural, racial, and power differences. We refer to trust as the *intangible* tangible in the fabric of human relationships. Trust is the thing that cannot be touched or seen, but it solidifies relationships among and between people establishing community, organizations, and institutions. Trust has been described as a state of expressed confidence and reliability in something or someone.

Covey (2006) offers a simple straightforward description of trust and how it manifests in our lives.

> Simply put, trust means confidence. The opposite of trust—distrust—is suspicion. When you trust people, you have confidence in them—in their integrity and in their abilities. When you distrust people, you are suspicious of them—of their integrity, their agenda, their capabilities, or their track record. (p. 5)

Trust describes a condition of the bond between or among people. This connection can be strong or weak, high or low, and any point in between. It signifies the level of cohesiveness within relationships. The level of trust in a relationship denotes how close or distant people are with one another. The level of closeness people maintain with each other dictates the ease of flow in and among lifeworld experiences.

What happens when trust is lost? In the pursuit of understanding the essence of trust, Larson and LaFasto (1989) take great care to display what might happen when trust is lost. They give an explanation of the level of trust by graphing its ebb and flow through moments of disappointment with effective, high-performing teams. They describe trust as a virtuous trait that is essential to bonding people and conclude that relationships are doomed to fail without trust. Their research of what makes effective high-performing teams revealed four essential operational principles:

> (1) honesty—integrity, no lies, no exaggerations; (2) openness—a willingness to share, and a receptivity to information, perceptions, ideas; (3) consistency—predictable behavior and responses; and, (4) respect—treating people with dignity and fairness. (p. 85)

Larson and LaFasto emphasize that a breach of any of these four principles by a team member leads to disappointment and severely compromises the group's trust. Figure 5.1 depicts a progression of what happens to trust levels when principles are violated.

Figure 5.1 **When Trust Is Broken**

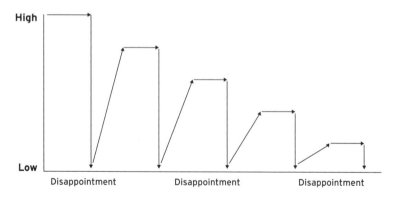

Source: Adapted from *TeamWork: What Must Go Right/What Can Go Wrong* by Carl E. Larson & Frank M. J. LaFasto, 1989. Newbury Park, CA: Sage. Used with permission.

Moving from left to right, the graphic shows a bar on the far left indicating a high level of trust. When a violation occurs, disappointment is introduced into the relationship and the level of confidence plummets from the highest point to the very lowest. Trust plummets when what was expected did not happen. For example, when your loved one doesn't explain and meets you for dinner three hours later than planned. Or, when you were scheduled to meet with your work group at 8:30 a.m. but no one notified you when the time changed to 11:30. In both cases the principles of honesty, openness, consistency, and respect are violated. What was agreed upon and expected did not happen. If the violation is not reconciled, over time trust will rise from this low point but will plateau at a much lower level and never reach its original high point. It simply sinks to a significantly lower, less trusting point than before. Any recurring violation eventually leads to more disappointment, which can be envisioned as a downward spiral to a collapsed relationship in which open engagement is all but impossible.

These simple examples demonstrate how violating principles of trust fractures the bond in a relationship, yet they pale in comparison to the generational breaches throughout U.S. history. Legalized enslavement followed by years of segregation and disenfranchisement served to institutionalize skepticism between African Americans and European Americans. Into the mix of breaches, add the practice of legally barring women from legislative process and economic prosperity; the seizure of properties of Japanese Americans and placing them in internment camps; the subjugation of Chinese Americans leaving them to suffer horrific working conditions and oppressive segregation; the abduction of land from Mexican Americans; the forced migration of First Nation people onto reservations while placing their children in boarding schools to make them more American; LGBTQ+ people forced to hide for fear of physical and psychological harm. For the most part, these violations go unreconciled, leaving trust levels at their lowest points.

Restoring Trust

When trust has been lost, can we get it back? The good news is that under the proper conditions, trust can be restored to its original value or reach new heights in the relationship. Here are conditions under which it can be resurrected.

Condition 1: Crisis. When in a crisis, people come together and form a tight bond to effectively handle the immediate emergency. You may be familiar with stories about estranged family members working together when one member needs critical health care. And, we've all witnessed communities joining together during and after natural disasters—and political adversaries joining forces to provide assistance in times of need (e.g., New Jersey Governor Christie and President Obama in the aftermath of Hurricane Sandy). The downside to trust restoration under crisis is that people tend to resume the lower trust levels after resolution.

Condition 2: Successfully working together. Trust can be restored when people work together and achieve a common goal. Success breeds success and fuels confidence. Confidence grows as people rely on one another more often and reliability is anticipated. Disappointments are replaced with accomplishments when expectations are met. A sense of attainment replaces doubt and restores faith. Over time, trust can be strengthened and accelerates until it is fully restored. Figure 5.2 shows that trust grows with each successful accomplishment.

Figure 5.2 **When Trust Is Regained**

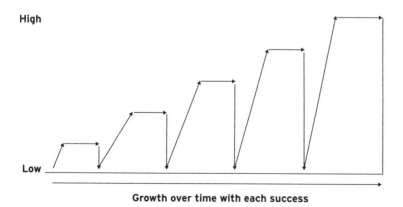

Growth over time with each success

Source: Adapted from *TeamWork: What Must Go Right/What Can Go Wrong* by Carl E. Larson & Frank M. J. LaFasto, 1989. Newbury Park, CA: Sage.

Condition 3: Forgiveness. Perhaps the most potent condition that leads to rapid trust restoration and new heights of trust is the act of forgiveness. Because of the magnitude of forgiveness in restoring relationships, it is worth a longer explanation. Keep in mind that forgiveness happens when the person who has been offended or violated releases all resentment for the transgression.

Madsen, Gygi, Hammond, and Plowman (2009) conducted extensive research to find a definition for forgiveness. They provide the following:

1. There is an injury or violation with subsequent emotional/physical pain.

2. The violation results in a broken/fragmented relationship between parties.

3. Perpetuation of injury is halted.

4. A cognitive process is pursued where the painful event or action is understood or reframed with a fuller context.

5. There is a release or letting go of justifiable emotion and retaliation related to the event.

6. There is a renegotiation of the relationship. (p. 249)

These elements outline the steps that occur during a breach and restoration of trust. Beginning with the injury through the point of renegotiation, we gain a clear view of what is required to move toward reconciliation. We add the crucial components of *acknowledgment* and *acceptance* of the breach by both parties. When the parties realize that a breach has occurred and acknowledge the role they played, they are able to engage in negotiation. Without acknowledgment and acceptance of involvement, trust further deteriorates and the relationship continues on the path to perdition.

Regaining Trust

Studying Figures 5.1 and 5.2, you see how trust is lost when promises are broken, leading to disappointment. Trust can be regained through focused efforts and purposeful actions. In this exercise, you will focus on the practice of forgiveness. It is our belief that you can't receive forgiveness if you are unwilling to practice forgiveness.

1. Think about someone who has deeply wronged you—someone you feel is impossible to forgive. When you think about this person, you experience pain, sadness, fear, and anger.

2. When you have identified that person, begin the process of forgiveness by composing a letter. Using that person's perspective, write a letter to yourself and ask for your forgiveness. Think about what you need to hear to promote healing. Think about what wrong needs to be acknowledged.

3. Begin the letter with a salutation "Dear [Your Name]," and be careful to write from the other person's perspective. In the body of the letter, write *everything* that you want that person to say to you.

4. Sign the letter from that person.

5. Read the letter to yourself every day. Reflect on the letter-writing experience using the following questions as guides:
   - What are you learning about forgiveness?
   - What did you notice about yourself before, during, and after you wrote the letter?
   - What was enlightening about this process?

6. When you no longer need to read the words, put the letter away in a safe place.

7. Destroy the letter when you have developed some distance from the initial writing and no longer need to read it to yourself.

8. Finally, allow time to reflect on the entire experience, choosing time intervals from the point you wrote the letter through the point you threw it away.

Shifting Experiences

Try This

It is our belief that storytelling can move mountains, though we aren't trying to move mountains here, just you! Your movement has far greater influence than the greatest of mountain chains. Sometimes you are unable to form words to detail what you are thinking, feeling, or experiencing. For this exercise, we selected a poem to guide a shift in perspective. The poem offers a common experience that we can share with others, giving us the opportunity to see how different people make various meanings from the same experience. This is an opportunity to synthesize content and experience from previous chapters. Consider your social cultural identity, how we communicate with each other, and the power that trust plays in relationships.

1. As you read the poem, underline words or phrases that resonate with you. We define *resonate* as something that deeply affects you, connects with you, or aligns with your values.

Judge Softly

Pray, don't find fault with the man that limps,
   Or stumbles along the road.
   Unless you have worn the moccasins he wears,
   Or stumbled beneath the same load.
There may be tears in his soles that hurt
   Though hidden away from view.
   The burden he bears placed on your back
   May cause you to stumble and fall, too.
Don't sneer at the man who is down today
   Unless you have felt the same blow
   That caused his fall or felt the shame
   That only the fallen know.
You may be strong, but still the blows
   That were his, unknown to you in the same way,
   May cause you to stagger and fall, too.
Don't be too harsh with the man that sins.
   Or pelt him with words, or stone, or disdain.
   Unless you are sure you have no sins of your own,
   And it's only wisdom and love that your heart contains.
For you know if the tempter's voice
   Should whisper as soft to you,
   As it did to him when he went astray,
   It might cause you to falter, too.
Just walk a mile in his moccasins
   Before you abuse, criticize and accuse.

If just for one hour, you could find a way

To see through his eyes, instead of your own muse.

I believe you'd be surprised to see

That you've been blind and narrow-minded, even unkind.

There are people on reservations and in the ghettos

Who have so little hope, and too much worry on their minds.

Brother, there but for the grace of God go you and I.

Just for a moment, slip into his mind and traditions

And see the world through his spirit and eyes

Before you cast a stone or falsely judge his conditions.

Remember to walk a mile in his moccasins

And remember the lessons of humanity taught to you by your elders.

We will be known forever by the tracks we leave

In other people's lives, our kindnesses and generosity.

Take the time to walk a mile in his moccasins.

—Mary T. Lathrap (1895)

2. Choose one or two of the words or phrases that you underlined and write a reflective response. Think about why that word or phrase is important and what it means to you. Think about how that word or phrase shows up in your actions.

3. Read the poem with a trusted friend, family member, or colleague. Invite your partner to read and underline meaningful phrases.

4. Share your phrases reflections with each other.

5. Share highlights from this chapter with your partner. Think about the following questions to guide your conversation:

- What are the implications for having conversations in a space of cross-social identities?
- In what ways do our actions support or go against the information in this chapter?
- What might be some purposeful actions that you will take as a result of reading this book?
- What validity claim (truth, rightness, truthfulness) can you identify that support underlining certain words or phrases?

6

Talk Before You Tackle

Oh Great Spirit, help me never judge another until
I have walked two weeks in their moccasins.

−often attributed as a Native American proverb

Sometimes understanding what we experience—what we hear or see—can be difficult. Because we filter new data through our lifeworld reservoir, which is filled with our own background information and experiences, we make sense of new encounters through old frames. This creates a condition whereby we hear or see with our ears and eyes but may not understand. Because we interpret everything through the lifeworld experience, at best we simply have the means of reaching common perspective on which we can agree. Consequently, understanding is a condition of reaching agreement about what is encountered.

To understand, we have to look and listen differently to recognize and process new data in new ways. Processing new information in new ways requires uncoupling from our current and background knowledge to gain a perspective of other possibilities.

Roy's Story

> Roy drove his pearl-white SUV to the dealership for an oil change, tire check, and brake inspection. Despite arriving early, he found a string of cars stretched around the building. Slightly deflated, he parked in the service line and handed his keys to the attendant. The congested waiting room, stocked with a coffee machine, water, and comfortable chairs, was centered around a big screen television. Composed, coffee in hand, he settled into a chair.

The lead story in the news chronicled an incident in which two young African American men were handcuffed, arrested, and removed from a coffee shop in Philadelphia (Siegel, 2018). The story was followed by another about a female African American graduate student taking a power nap in the commons area of an Ivy League dormitory between cramming for exams. A white student reported her presence as "suspicious" to the campus police department, which then dispatched officers to question her (Caron, 2018).

Roy wondered what was at the root of these events. Glancing around, he suddenly realized he was the only white person in the room. Everyone else seemed to be part of the story, heads nodding in unison at key points. Roy's relaxed calm faded and he slowly pulled his body to attention in the chair. He realized that this was the first time in his life that he was the only white man in a room that was filled with people. He became emotionally overwhelmed at the thought of being the "only." Although no one showed aggression toward him, he felt judged. He decided to break the ice and make small talk with people near him. He was surprised to discover they shared many commonalities, beyond just working nearby.

When the attendant signaled that his car was ready, Roy walked to the cashier and completed the easy transaction with the slide of his credit card. Keys in hand, he turned to leave the waiting room. He stopped near the cashier's desk when he noticed a different reality operating at the other cashier's desk. Roy watched as an African American man, about his age, attempted to pay for services. The cashier questioned the man's form of payment and asked for his identification, address, and phone number. Roy hadn't been asked for any of that information. What took Roy less than a minute was requiring a tremendous amount of time and effort by this other man. Roy became upset and then downright angry at a much deeper level. He wondered how this difference in how he and the African American man were treated could be happening in the United States. Even more so, how was it that he had never noticed these inequities before?

Roy now realized that he was not being judged by the other customers. But he acknowledged the void between them—Roy had not known what was painfully obvious to everyone else: freedom and justice for all really stood for freedom and justice for some.

Although Roy left the dealership without remark, it is clear that the opportunity for a changed perspective is well within his grasp. His lifeworld now includes an unreconciled disturbance that reminds him that the world he thought he knew and trusted is more tenuous than what he understood it to be.

A Second Look

Remember the illusion of the artwork that shows a young woman—or an old woman? See Figure 6.1. If you focus on the chin just above the fur line of a coat, you will see a young woman with her face slightly turned away. Her nose and cheek are in view, with an eyelash just below her hairline. A plume sits on her head, in front of a decorative scarf that partially covers her hair as it flows onto her shoulder.

A second look may conjure an entirely different image. Just below the chin area of the young woman, notice the mouth of an older woman. The older woman's eye emerges from what was the younger woman's ear. The decorative head scarf now appears as a shawl that drapes the older woman's head and shoulders.

Next, consider how this illusion was viewed by Inuit children in one of our workshops. They eagerly pointed out the figures of a badger and a polar bear, both familiar to their lifeworld experiences. The dark area atop the young woman's head, often identified as hair, is a badger burrowing down into a snow cave. And the polar bear rests at the top of the picture, with his nose pointed toward the plume and his body draped down the rear of the image. From an entirely different lifeworld experience, one of our workshop participants who works at an impoverished inner-city school promptly identified the "badger" as a large rat burrowing in a hole.

Figure 6.1 **Illusions Shaped by Lifeworld**

Simply, we bring our background knowledge and information from our subconscious to our consciousness when making sense of what is in front of us. Although each observer saw the same picture, they made sense of the image using their own frames of reference. It is safe to say that we make sense of what we see in the moment based upon prior experiences. What is behind us informs what is in front of us.

Processing New Experiences

Sometimes hearing and seeing isn't enough for us to process a new experience. In some cases, you may need a disturbance forceful enough to loosen old lifeworld references. A crisis in your ability to make sense of a situation activates the realignment of neural pathways in your brain so you can address what is in front of you. What old neural associations do not recognize, new ones define. In Roy's case, the trip to the crowded dealership placed him in a situation with enough disturbance to shift his attention to something that had been slightly beyond his normal field of vision. He witnessed an African American audience nod in agreement to the obvious mistreatment of two young African American men in a Philadelphia coffeehouse. His curiosity was just enough to wonder why he did not nod in unison with the rest of the customers. That helped him identify as an outsider, which meant seeking to understand what the insiders knew placed him in a mini-crisis. Just enough disturbance flooded his field of vision to create a space that allowed him to witness the multiple realities for U.S. citizens—the *haves* and the *have nots*. As a member of the haves, he witnessed himself moving through a world buoyed by social benefits that enhance his experience as a citizen. He had assumed that these benefits were offered to all. Now he knows differently.

Truthfully, it is difficult to see new truths through the prism of old beliefs. As one participant stated in a recent workshop, "As an entitled white male in this country, I wake up every day and see the world as my oyster. I've never experienced [my world] as a nightmare."

Seeing What Is Hidden

We have taken on a task of constructing a pathway where conversations lead beyond established constructs of race, class, gender, age, ableness, poverty, class, sexual orientation, and many of the *negative beliefs* that currently classify power stratifications in U.S. society. We have witnessed individuals and groups engage in authentic dialogue about the meanings of these long-standing classifications. Over time, they gain clarity about these language constructs as means to segregate, subjugate, and subordinate. They further understand the notion of privilege and entitlement as an accrued benefit given to a few to the detriment of others.

Authentic conversations in which participants are able to describe reality in unequitable terms creates the opportunity to imagine a world that is unshackled from traditional constructs of power. Through these discussions, we discover that to envision an equitable society in which fairness and justice are discernable, we must uncover current inequities within our work spaces. To pass beyond age discrimination, we need to see how we currently construct age. To get beyond gender bias, we need to see how we currently construct gender. To move beyond racism, we need to see how we currently construct race. This list of inequities needs to be expanded to include every one of the "-isms" that we place in the politically correct bin.

In our workshops, participants soon determine that taking risk is instrumental for mindful conversations. Personal and professional participation in maintaining and propagating unfairness is explored. They tackle fundamental questions that must be answered by anyone serious about holding authentic conversations leading to an equitable society:

1. How do I come to see what is hidden in plain view?
2. What conditions create enough disturbance to unfasten my perspective from the privilege and entitlement that are harbored in my lifeworld experience?

Amending Entitlement

In a quest for justice, we are compelled to recognize that oppressed groups seeking equality need to be amended into the U.S. Constitution. On the other hand, heterosexual white men as a group, the unstated norm, have never needed to be amended into the Constitution. Whether consciously or unconsciously, they have enjoyed power, as manifested in the form of privilege or entitlement, as part of our history and economic status in this country (CampbellJones, 2002, p. 14).

In Brenda's dissertation, *Against the Stream: White Men Who Act in Ways to Eradicate Racism and White Privilege/Entitlement in the United States of America* (2002), she presents compelling research about key elements needed to unhinge from current worldviews so that it becomes possible to see something different. Her study focused on influential heterosexual white males who intentionally worked to dismantle racism.

Her contention is simple: When things work to your benefit, they are invisible to you. You do not experience them as an advantage, but as the norm of how things are for everyone. And, because of your advantaged circumstance, you do not pay attention to what is not working well, particularly as it relates to others. Things are simply the way they should be, and there is no need to change things for the better.

Even the most advantaged members of society benefit from learning about the privilege that accrues as a result of their entitled positions. It serves to make them more responsive and responsible members of society. However, knowledge and understanding of this endemic problem is not enough. Otherwise, the laws would have changed the injustices that have hurt millions of lives in the United States.

If laws do not make the change for an equitable society, what does? Or more to the point, who does? Brenda concludes that societal change happens through the actions of people within the society itself. She further argues that the most entitled must be at the forefront of equitable change using their entitled position in society to leverage change. But, how do members of the entitled and privileged position themselves for equitable action to ensure the U.S. ideal of equality?

As stated in the coauthored book *The Cultural Proficiency Journey: Moving Beyond Ethical Barriers Toward Profound School Change* (2010), Brenda's research described five critical elements that were operational in the lives of the men studied who self-identify as benefiting from white privilege:

1. Each man had a relationship with a significant person early in life where the principle of "the golden rule" of reciprocity was central to their teaching. This principle became the moral anchor for all intentional actions for eradicating racism.

2. Each experienced a racial dilemma triggering a critical emotional event that tested their commitment to this principle. Their ability to act congruently with the principle triggered a snowballing effect reinforcing further consistent behaviors.

3. Each man consciously took intentional action to eradicate racial injustice, given they were immersed in an environment of privilege and entitlement leading them to experience competing values that suggested they enjoy these benefits. They consciously dismissed privileged situations and sought to elevate those historically disenfranchised in society.

4. Each man had a relationship with someone at the receiving end of social injustice, in all cases African American men. They clearly understood their unique position of being blind to privilege because they benefited from privileged perspectives, acts, policies, and structures in society. They trusted and relied upon the perspectives and the experiences of others not receiving benefits to be their cross-cultural informants—to help them see what they could not see.

5. Each man engaged in a process of critical reflective analysis. They constantly participated in critical self-critique relative to their principle—the golden rule—and their action. (p. 65)

In her research, Brenda reported that each participant in the study experienced a significant emotional event placing them in crisis that forced them to "see where they were once blind" to what was around them (p. 93). Brenda says that by seeing, these men were able to realign their actions with core principles that were set early in their lives. Just as Roy experienced a vision realignment at the dealership, so did the men in her study.

See the model of Intentional Moral Action for Racial Justice in Figure 6.2, which displays the key elements operating fluidly and dynamically. The moral principles are positioned in the center of the model, establishing parameters that guide social justice activity. Justice, equity, and the golden rule of reciprocity are the three pillars that inform all intentional equitable acts.

Entering the throes of equity activism requires alignment with your *cor*, founded in justice and fairness. Anyone cocooned in a privileged world needs to answer this question: *Why should I disrupt my daily experience of realizing the benefits of the haves on behalf of creating fairness for the have-nots?* The men studied found it necessary to make equity activism a conscious decision, because subconsciously and traditionally, they were accustomed to doing the opposite. They entered into activism when prompted by a critical life disturbance that rattled their privileged lifeworld reference points, causing them to shift focus, realign with core principles, and make course corrections. They discovered that their lives were not sullied for doing equity work. But rather, their lifeworlds were enriched, their vision made clear, and their lives became more purposeful.

Figure 6.2 **Intentional Moral Action for Racial Justice**

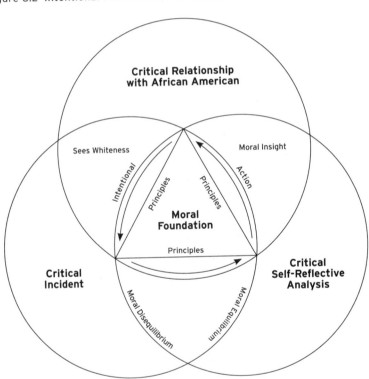

Try
This

Shifting Perceptions

When in a critical conversation, everyone shifts perceptions among three different points of view. These points of view are first-person "I," second-person "you," and third-person "observer." Becoming familiar with these varying points of view is central to understanding how your group reaches agreement and how your perceptual horizon expands. A healthy exercise is to deliberately assume the perceptual perspective of each point of view to gain insight into varying worldviews.

For example, if participating in a conversation focused on understanding assigned gender perspectives, it would be beneficial to take on gender social issues from each point of view as "first," "second," or "third" person. Consider the following: If you self-identified as gender *straight,* take on a point of view of the gender identification *lesbian.* From this perspective, consider the process of enrolling your child into a kindergarten class in a traditional (straight) school community. What challenges or opportunities might you encounter in this role? Consider the same situation from the second person "you" perspective with the self-identified gender straight school staff. What challenges or opportunities might be present for a family desiring to enroll their child in your school? As a third-person observer, self-identified gender straight person, what would you most likely witness in this scenario?

From each perspective, you would experience the same situation very differently. This exercise allows you to experience the difference in perceptions and gain an appreciation for that difference. It is in understanding and appreciating the difference that cross-cultural communication thrives. If you have difficulty performing this exercise, ask *why* to extend your understanding of your current boundaries.

Although the example provides practice around potential issues associated with gender identification, this exercise can easily be applied to conversations you and your colleagues have about poverty, social class, race, xenophobia, and any other topics that connote social power differentials. The point is to gain perspective from multiple reference points and expand your lifeworld data bank, enabling competent conversation about topics that are generally regarded to be difficult.

This experience asks you to move among perceptual perspectives to gain insight into varying worldviews. Next, we'll ask you to put yourself into unfamiliar physical spaces. Experience a few hours—or longer—in an environment where you are not among the cultural majority:

- NABSA conference (National Association of Black School Administrators)
- Black hair salon
- Supermarket (not in your neighborhood)
- Gay Pride parade
- Temple, mosque, synagogue, or church (visit a variety of faith-based places of worship)
- Inner-city emergency room
- Region(s) of the country unfamiliar to you
- Rural or urban community

7

Uncover Values and Perspectives

To believe in something, and not to live it, is dishonest.
–Mahatma Gandhi

We invite you to join us in imagining a society where productive conversations about race, class, gender, culture, and poverty are the norm and can be facilitated by examining and exposing inequities. As much as you may experience external constraints to social mobility, understanding the subjective foundations for those restrictions moves us toward new possibilities.

Chris Argyris (1990) developed the Ladder of Inference model to show how our background shapes our behavior. Steps on the ladder illustrate how internal, invisible processes facilitate the occurrence of observable actions or behaviors. The steps of the ladder indicate the subjective processing used to undergird and justify objective actions. Argyris's model proposes that it is possible to understand what lies beneath tangible acts. He contends that our values, beliefs, and assumptions shape our conclusions, which ultimately inform what we come to believe about the world around us. The belief becomes the guiding principle that governs actions. Extending Argyris's original model, Senge (1990) contends that beliefs possess the power to determine the data you select. Beliefs essentially dictate your field of vision and filter new data, essentially hampering your ability to perceive anything new. The consequence of filtering actively limits your ability to experience any new data you encounter. In short, we see through our beliefs.

Consider the following illustration of how values, assumptions, and beliefs shape the world we perceive. We facilitate an exercise during workshops in which participants are randomly partnered to dialogue. Our specific purpose is to place participants in a safe structure where there is a high probability for surfacing values, assumptions, and beliefs. One pairing was a middle-aged white female with a 25-year-old white male. She wore professionally tailored clothing with matching leather pumps. His dress was casual and he wore his hair in a long ponytail. During the whole group sharing at the end of the pairing exercise, she tearfully shared the following:

> When I was first paired with my partner, I thought he was some marijuana hippie-type person. I really didn't want to be his partner. But as luck would have it, I was assigned to him. Based on his looks, I figured he liked to party and have a good time. I assumed he hung around others who did the same. Probably jobless or in a low-paying job, I wondered "How does he afford to stay high all the time? Why is he here, anyway, practicing skills we had learned earlier in the seminar?" Our dialogue revealed that he had just graduated from college and had been admitted to a master's program. I'm ashamed of myself for all the things I assumed about this wonderful young man. I also learned that he was growing his hair for cancer victims and has been donating his long locks for wigs since he was a teenager. He is due for a head shave at the end of the week. Had I not had this conversation and raised questions about what I believed I saw in him, I would have continued to hold erroneous assumptions about him and men with long hair.

Pulling Aside the Curtain

Recall *The Wizard of Oz,* in which young Dorothy is taken away from the safe and familiar surroundings of her Kansas farm by a ferocious tornado. She is deposited in an unfamiliar place, fraught with the dangers of a wicked witch, flying monkeys, and challenging landscapes filled with dangerous beasts. As Dorothy travels the yellow brick road in search of the wizard who holds the key to returning her to Kansas, she befriends a scarecrow, a tin man, and a lion. Her new friends achieve intelligence, a heart, and courage. They discover these possibilities were within their grasp all along, but only after the wizard was disclosed as a fake by Toto. Looking inward allowed the characters to see what was within them. Dorothy eventually gets her wish of returning home with three heel clicks of her ruby red pumps while repeatedly chanting, "There's no place like home." Upon awakening, she discovers that she never left Kansas. A bump on her head and little journey down a yellow brick road gave her the courage to face her fears.

When we pull open our minds to explore the foundation of our actions, we begin to understand how seemingly objective acts are built upon subjective reasoning. As Dorothy discovered, we too have not quite reached Oz. The great reveal, as Dorothy discovered, is that we take ourselves with us wherever we go. In the workshop scenario, the woman shared her proclivity toward making snap judgments about others. She is not alone. It is safe to say that we all engage in making decisions about others within nanoseconds—whether we meet them or observe them. In his book *Blink,* Malcolm Gladwell (2005) makes the case for our need to make snap decisions and their importance as equal to our need to make more thoughtfully deliberated decisions (p. 15). Our position is that all decisions, whether fast or slow, are loaded with assumptions and that understanding those assumptions leads to discovery of what we value.

Values

Uncovering what is valued discloses how we assign importance to what is ultimately viewed as objective observable data. Seeing the assigned importance to what we value reveals the foundation that undergirds all assumptions, shapes conclusions, and constructs our beliefs, which ultimately govern action. For example, most of us have deeply woven subconscious values including family, peace, and hard work. These aspects of morality function in the background, and are mostly taken for granted as we go about our daily routines (Heidegger, Macquarrie, & Robinson, 1968; Schein, 2004). These values are essential in shaping how we govern our lives and interact with others.

Acknowledging and knowing the experiences that construct our own values helps us to understand that someone else, with a different lifeworld, may have different values. For example, how you value family is based upon early experiences with caregivers who shaped your sense of appreciation of the *idea* of family. Each person brings their idea of family expressed as a value, though shaped by different or similar experiences. It is entirely possible for two people to be in the same space and hold the same values, yet experience two completely different realities.

Climbing the Ladder of Inference

We often take action on the basis of split-second judgment, so how do we slow down processing to glimpse what is happening behind the curtains of actions and behavior? Let's take a closer look at how our values and beliefs affect what data we select, the meaning we make of them, and our subsequent action. Figure 7.1 illustrates the Ladder of Inference, a model first developed by Chris Argyris (1990) and then expanded by Peter Senge and his colleagues (Senge, Kleiner, Roberts, Ross, & Smith, 1994). The idea is to illustrate how an individual's observable action might be traced as steps associated with subjective processing. Imagine starting from the bottom step of a ladder and climbing to the top. We describe each step here beginning from the bottom.

Step 1: Available Data. Step 1 resides in the vast amounts of information ubiquitous within our daily lives. Valueless, it encompasses all observable data and actual experience, as captured by a device such as a video camera or digital recorder. For example, with a quick scan of your current surroundings, you'll find mounds of data around you. Windows, lamps, sounds, lighting, floors, and a table are potential data points. Also, include your emotional or physical state (e.g., body temperature, excitement about what you're learning, hunger, drowsiness). In a classroom, data might include pictures on the walls, sounds from the playground, bells ringing, and announcements.

Figure 7.1 **Ladder of Inference with Critical Questions**

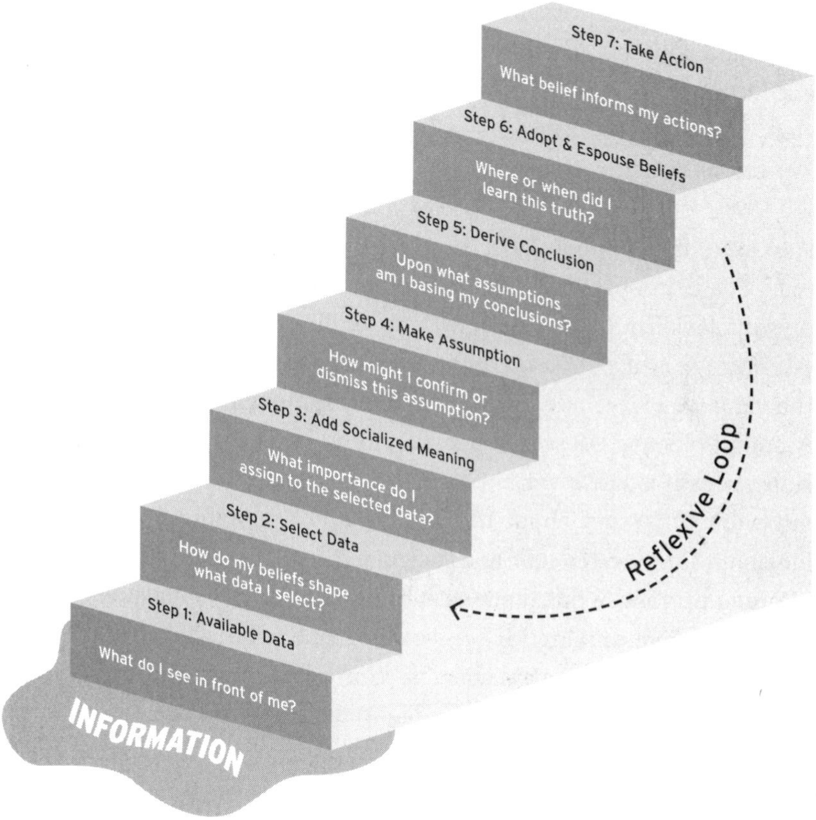

Step 7: Take Action
What belief informs my actions?
Step 6: Adopt & Espouse Beliefs
Where or when did I learn this truth?
Step 5: Derive Conclusion
Upon what assumptions am I basing my conclusions?
Step 4: Make Assumption
How might I confirm or dismiss this assumption?
Step 3: Add Socialized Meaning
What importance do I assign to the selected data?
Step 2: Select Data
How do my beliefs shape what data I select?
Step 1: Available Data
What do I see in front of me?
INFORMATION
Reflexive Loop

Source: © 2019 Faith CampbellJones. Adapted from P. M. Senge, A. Kleiner, C. Roberts, R. B. Ross, & B. J. Smith, *The Fifth Discipline Fieldbook: Strategies and Tools for Building a Learning Organization,* 1994, p. 243. New York: Doubleday/Currency.

Step 2: Select Data. The second step from the bottom represents data you select based upon what you *believe* to be important. This is a significant step. Although other data are present and readily available, this step is where you focus on what is important. Once this focus is achieved, all other data becomes invisible (we discuss more about invisibility in step 6). For example, you may not be focusing on a distant sound, paying attention to the lighting in the room, or thinking about the positioning of your body in chair. That data may be deselected because you have given your attention to the text.

Step 3: Add Socialized Meaning. You add cultural or socialized meaning as you interpret data through your own lens. Assigning importance and appreciation to the data based upon your socialized experience is an expressed value because what you value springs from this step. This is where terms like "good," "bad," "ugly," and "nice" emerge. For example, if you are paying attention to the chair, you notice that it is a "comfortable" chair. This is how you express a value about an object such as a chair. You may label the noise from the playground as "annoying." The list of cultural value characterizations is endless depending on your socialized association with the data.

Step 4: Make Assumptions. You form assumptions based upon the value you have assigned to the data, using your socialized prism. Assumptions are guesses you make about what direction or conclusion you will make, given the data you have selected. For example, in our workshop story about the woman and the young man with the long hair, she selected hair and assigned it to a negative value based on her assumptions about the length of hair for men. Consequently, she assumed that any male with long hair is bound to be lazy and spends his time and money on marijuana. The most important thing to remember about this step is that *all* people unavoidably make assumptions. However, the good news is that assumptions can be critiqued, and their accuracy confirmed or dismissed through conversational dialogue and critical questioning.

Step 5: Derive Conclusions. You draw conclusions based upon the assumptions you make and arrive at a decision. For example, because the woman in the workshop assumed the young man was a lazy marijuana user, she may believe that all young men with long hair are unintelligent and aren't making a positive contribution to society. However, if she assigns a positive value to long hair on young men, she may have assumed that the young man with long hair was intelligent and hard-working. After all, he was at the same seminar as she was. A logical conclusion would be that young men with long hair are as intelligent as she perceives herself to be.

Step 6: Adopt and Espouse Beliefs. Beliefs are principles that guide the way you live. They are generally applied as a framework to govern actions. Principles are powerful aspects of our socialization and have values and assumptions we conclude to be true. For example, you may *value* mutual respect. You *assume* that being respectful is an important way to engage in relationships. Therefore, you *conclude* that others are respectful as well. A belief that may arise from this value: *Do to others as you would have them do to you.* Our beliefs hold tremendous power. They specifically determine what data are selected from the vast pool of information that surrounds us. As illustrated by the reflexive loop displayed in Figure 7.1, beliefs can short-circuit the process and elim-inate considering all the data (step 1). How many times have you *not* seen the milk carton in the refrigerator because it is not in the place you *believed* it should be? When another person shows you that it was in plain view, you are shocked and embarrassed. Because your beliefs shape what data you select, it is difficult or impossible to see what you do not believe.

Step 7: Take Action. You act based upon what you believe to be true. Generally, you look at the action and not the belief that undergirds the action. For instance, if the action taken is that students must attend Saturday school for being tardy three or more times, critiquing the act of sending students to Saturday school does not make this action more effective for a change in student behavior. However, critiquing the belief that undergirds the need for Saturday school is much more effective. The question is "What do we believe about sending students to Saturday school?" If you don't pose this underlying question, you are likely to continue the practice of Saturday school. Until the belief behind the action is identified and analyzed, real change cannot occur. Effective sustainable change occurs beneath the action at the belief level.

Actions Spring from Beliefs

The Ladder of Inference becomes a powerful instrument for viewing how actions are born from beliefs—through which you construct reality. Values shape assumptions, which in turn inform conclusions that ultimately formulate beliefs. If behaving differently is the objective, simply adding more data without critiquing the belief as to why the data were selected distorts the process and leads to a high probability of obtaining the same results.

Let's apply the Ladder of Inference. A workshop participant shared his movement up the Ladder of Inference as he interacted with a student. The teacher ultimately took action based on his own *unexamined* assumptions. Keep in mind that we all take the journey up and down the ladder—adults and students.

Step 1: I observe data as a video-recording device would view it, without value placement. On the first day of class, the teacher enters the room and observes that he has 20 students, all seated at their desks.

Step 2: I select data from what I observe. The teacher observes Kaylan. She is sitting at her desk with a pencil and has her notebook open. This is the only observable data available to the teacher.

Step 3: I apply a culturally understood meaning to the data. The teacher gives cultural meaning to the data: He assigns Kaylan to the student demographic group Asian. His thought is that "Asian students love math and come ready to learn." The teacher values students who come ready to learn.

Step 4: I make assumptions based upon the meaning. The teacher assumes, "Asians are good at math. Kaylan must love math too, and she is ready to learn."

Step 5: I draw conclusions. The teacher resolves that Kaylan wants to learn in his class and will do well in math.

Step 6: I adopt beliefs about the world. The teacher believes that Asian students and students associated with Kaylan are serious about school and most likely good students.

Step 7: I take actions based upon my belief. The teacher works hard to be sure that his expectations of Kaylan are met regardless of whether Kaylan really likes math.

Making assumptions and moving up and down the Ladder of Inference is something we all do. It happens quickly and automatically, undetected as background processing. Given the pervasiveness of cultural biases—a natural and normal state of mind—it is crucial that assumptions are tested for accuracy by asking critical questions to interrupt the automaticity of the process. For example, in Step 4, the teacher assumed Kaylan loved mathematics. The teacher could test this assumption by raising the critical question, *How might I confirm or dismiss this assumption?* Talking with Kaylan about her favorite subjects in school might be the good starting point. Perhaps Kaylan does not like math at all and has never been good at it. The notebook she brought to class may be her writing journal. Perhaps she loves to write. Kaylan's response to the teacher's questions and assessments could easily change the teacher's conclusion, affecting his belief and ultimately how he interacts with her.

The reflexive loop on the Ladder of Inference in Figure 7.1 illustrates an automatic feedback process beginning with step 6 of adopted and espoused beliefs and it circles back to step 2 where data are selected. The model shows that we tend to pay attention to data that supports what we already believe and ignore other data from step 1. What we believe becomes our truth, leaving us to disregard information that contradicts it. As a result, we do not see any new information available to us. For example, armed with the belief that Kaylan is a good student, the teacher scans for any data that reinforces his belief and readily uses it to undergird his position. In turn, Kaylan travels the ladder and responds to the teacher by becoming interested in math. Her newfound interest reinforces the teacher's belief and establishes a positive value for math within her own belief system—a self-fulfilling prophecy. The same processing would happen were the teacher armed with the belief that Kaylan was not a good student. The outcome may be her failure in the subject. Eventually, as beliefs become more rigid, our perspective narrows, causing less attention to be given to other possible information sources. Simply adding new data in step 1 and leaving assumptions unquestioned is a recipe for failure. The belief becomes the truth, creating the situation of viewing other information, regardless of convincing arguments, through a distorted prism.

Creating Critical Questions

The reflexive loop indicated by the dotted line in Figure 7.1 illustrates our automatic tendency to support current actions that were selected from available data. The underlying intent is to validate old ways of doing things, particularly things judged to be working to our benefit. However, this processing leads to narrow-mindedness, which leaves us more likely to exclude other data. Under these conditions, our inability to see other possibilities makes the prospects of creating or maintaining an inclusive community impossible.

Questioning what you believe about your subjective processing holds the key to interrupting the cycle long enough for you to consider what other data best inform what and how you do things. For all practical purposes, other data do not exist because you have actively reselected information that supports the belief by searching the data field and actively choosing what best fits (Bellinger, 2004; CampbellJones, CampbellJones, & Lindsey, 2010). This simple but powerful observation is key to understanding why there are nagging gaps in education between demographic groups. For example, when a teacher believes that a select group of children belongs in honors courses, she selects data that supports recruiting and registering those children for the classes. Furthermore, throughout the program of study, she alters her pedagogy to ensure their success in mastering the course content. Conversely, if the same teacher believes that a select group of children does not belong in honors courses, she spends significant energy ensuring that those students do not enter the course. And if, for some reason, a child from the undesirable group slips through the crack and enters the class, the teacher diligently works at removing that student from the course. Students are not immune from this reflexive processing where beliefs govern what supporting data they select. Many African American and Latino students deselect themselves from entering advanced mathematics and science courses because they adopt the belief that they do not belong in the class, regardless of their proven intellectual aptitude for the subject (Ferguson, 2003; Grissom & Redding, 2016).

How do you interrupt the unconscious reflexive tendency to select data that support the way you always do things? As mentioned earlier, posing critical questions interrupts automatic processing by creating a space of possibility. This space affords greater data gathering in step 1 of the process. Note that Figure 7.1 has critical questions below each step. Use these questions as a guide to the type of questions needed at each step. Let's review the teacher's story about Kaylan, applying critical questions at each step in the process. How might the outcome change?

Step 1: I observe data, as a video recorder would view it. On the first day of class, the teacher enters the room and observes 20 students seated at their desks. *Critical questions:* What is in front of me that I cannot see because of my beliefs? What do I see?

Step 2: I select data from what I observe. One student, Kaylan, is Asian. *Critical questions:* Why did I select this data? What do I believe that caused me to select this data?

Step 3: I apply a culturally understood meaning to the data. "Asian students love math and come ready to learn." The teacher values students who come ready to learn and are good in mathematics. *Critical questions:* Why are these data important to me? From whom did I learn that these data were important?

Step 4: I make assumptions based upon the meaning. The teacher assumes, "Asians are good in math. Kaylan must love school and love math." *Critical questions:* How might I confirm or dismiss this assumption? What assumptions am I making based upon what I value?

Step 5: I draw conclusions. The teacher concludes that Kaylan wants to learn in his class and will do well in math. *Critical questions:* Upon what assumptions am I basing my conclusions? Are the conclusions consistent with what I value?

Step 6: I adopt beliefs about the world. The teacher believes that any other Asian student and any student associated with Kaylan are serious about school and most likely good math students. *Critical questions:* From whom did I learn this belief? Where or when did I learn this truth? Does this belief still serve me well today?

Step 7: I take actions based upon my belief. The teacher works hard to be sure that his expectations of Kaylan are met regardless of whether Kaylan really likes math. *Critical questions:* What do I believe about this action? Why is this action important to me?

Asking critical questions of one another or journaling responses to questions has a huge bearing on how you see the world and respond to others. When questioning the assumption at Step 4, simply asking Kaylan what her favorite subject is in school or what she likes most about school gives you access to learn that perhaps she does not like school at all. Perhaps physical education or reading is her favorite subject, or Kaylan may confirm that she does like math. Kaylan's response to any of these questions could easily change the teacher's conclusion, affecting his belief and ultimately his actions. Not examining values, assumptions, and ultimately our beliefs, could lead to dire consequences for relationships. Whereas questioning them leads to strong and healthy relationships.

Breaking with tradition and critically questioning what we believe, assume, and value is a crucial step in moving conversations beyond race, class, culture, and social status. When we take the step of coming out from hiding in plain view, we open to what is possible. It is the focus on what is possible that leads from describing an old, exclusive world to describing a new, inclusive society.

Using the Ladder of Inference

1. Using this example as a model, craft an example of how you apply the Ladder of Inference in your personal or professional life. Read the model upward beginning with Step 1.

Step 7: I take actions based upon my beliefs.
- I avoid interaction with veteran teachers in the teachers' lounge.

Step 6: I adopt and espouse beliefs about the world.
- I follow the rule of keeping my head low before speaking out to those in the know.

Step 5: I draw conclusions.
- It is best to lay low until I earn my stripes for entry into the club.

Step 4: I make assumptions based upon the meaning I added.
- Not receiving an open invitation is a signal to stay away and not enter the group.

Step 3: I add meaning based upon my socialization.

- I appreciate an invitation to join an established group.

Step 2: I select data from what I observe.

- Veteran teachers cluster together with new teachers scattered around the room.

Step 1: I observe data and experiences as captured by a recording device.

1. Teachers assemble in the teachers' lounge before class and during lunch break.

2. Share your example with a trusted friend, colleague, or family member. Ask your partner for feedback.

3. Reflect on this process, using these guiding questions:
- What was this process like for you?
- What was easy about this process?
- What was hard about this process?
- How can you apply this process to your life, classroom, or work environment?

8

Question with
Better Questions

Listening… requires not only open
eyes and ears, but open hearts and minds.
–Lisa Delpit *(1995, p. 46)*

In the previous chapters, we asked you to move beyond the superficial conversation that may be typical in your daily professional or personal relationships. We emphasized participating in dialogues that evoke possibility and generosity and invited you to commit to skill development by having a level of authentic conversational praxis with others using the exercises at the end of each chapter. Now, we will explore the power of questions as central to authentic conversations.

According to Peter Block (2008), raising the question is the most provocative aspect of building relations in community. "Questions," he writes, "are more transformative than answers and are the essential engagement tools" (p. 103). Block echoes the earlier observations of

Paulo Freire (Freire & Shor, 1987) concerning nurturing curiosity in learning. Freire emphasized the power of questioning for teachers.

> An education of answers does not at all help the curiosity that is indispensable in the cognitive process.... Only an education of questions can trigger, motivate, and reinforce curiosity. (p. 31)

We concur with Freire and Block and advocate for participating in a conversation of questions as a means of approaching transformative equitable change. Our position is that relationships are too important and central to what makes community and, by extension, organizations such as schools. We generate possibility through conversational inquiry rather than simply relying on dictates or mandates for action. It is through cocreating possibility that the potential for something new emerges.

Questions are intended to open up what is possible rather than shut down the emergence of newness. Questions give us the opportunity to imagine what is possible for the potential of a newly created world. Asking questions gives unimaginable opportunities to forge new understandings within existing relationships and to cocreate new understandings.

Provocative Questions

We experience culture as a dominant force in our lives, giving us structure that expresses values, assumptions, and beliefs. Exploring and challenging deeply held values and assumptions that may be barriers to equity becomes possible when inquisitiveness becomes a central mindset. Inquisitiveness is crucial to achieving authentic relationships. Whether maintaining the consensus of values and beliefs you currently realize or forming new ones, constructing *different* relationships are facilitated through raising questions—more so than providing answers. Thus, questions are central to your examination of values, assumptions, and beliefs. Questions have the propensity for building strong relationships with people whose cultures may be different than your own.

Good questions help to bring our values and assumptions to the foreground, where they can be critically examined. Although pulling values and assumptions that work for us into the foreground is extremely taxing work, it is necessary. Good questions have the power to interrupt the internal processing that creates a slight pause in automatic action. They provoke what is possible rather than reinforce what already exists. Good questions spark the future and liberate us from the past.

When posing questions, we want to be sure we do not seek to control the response, such as when using a question beginning with "Don't you think...?" As soon as you insert what you want the person to think, it not only requires a yes or no answer but leads them to a predetermined response. When asking such questions, possibility is closed down. Similarly, asking questions that assume you have the power to change another person's actions signals domination and should be avoided. Examples of such questions would be those beginning with the stem "How do we get them to...?" Although the questions may sound robust, they are powerless and weak. They presuppose that the person asking the questions already has the answer.

Weak questions assume you have the power to change something (or anything) else about someone other than you. Weak questions leave you out of the equation, by not treating the one making the inquiry as part of the relationship. In their discussion of culturally proficient learning communities, Lindsey and colleagues (2009) provide excellent guidelines to help you recognize weak questions. Similar to Block, they argue that weak, unproductive questions should be avoided in the process of cocreating stronger relationships. They suggest discontinuing use of powerless questions because they

1. Have the answers embedded in the question:
   — Have you thought about...?
   — Did you think about...?
2. Imply judgment and blame:
   — Did you realize the effect you were having on those students?
3. Generate pressure and defensiveness:
   — Why did you do it that way?

Robust or powerful questions, on the other hand, invite a sense of familiarity and free the people involved to work collaboratively and creatively. Such questions draw you from the sidelines and place you center stage—as actor rather than spectator.

We create the world in which we live. When we realize the power we each hold in the words we speak, we have the power to change the world we have created for ourselves. A powerful question consists of the following qualities:

1. It is open-ended. Questions that require a yes or no answer do not allow for the responding person to examine personal values, beliefs, and assumptions. There is no opportunity for the person to share personal meaning.

2. It is provocative. It interrupts the persons's thinking and causes disequilibrium. It's at this point that there is a greater possibility for learning and insight.

3. It evokes passion. Stimulating passion leads to conviction. Conviction is aroused by passion and commitment is attained. Creating a space for the personal allows the person to make connections to what is important to them.

Robust questions open possibility. Consider the following:

- What do you value that caused you to attend the meeting?
- What commitment are you willing to make to the success of the effort?
- What is the answer the problem is imploring you to discover?

Creating Powerful Questions

The mindset of the person posing a question erects a platform that determines how we talk with one another (Block, 2008). Entering the conversational space with a mindset that holds everyone in esteem extends an invitation for discovery of what's possible. When we value what each person has to offer and are ready to be influenced by someone else's perspective, personal visions have the potential to converge. Shared visions offer enhanced perspectives and lead to deeper understanding of yourself and others as you work toward fostering a consensual and just world.

When formulating questions, keep in mind the goal of opening up future possibilities within the relationship instead of closing them down. The inquiry does not seek answers that offer quick results but rather sets the conversationalists on an investigative, transformative path where the end result is a deep, purposeful commitment to the relationship. With that said, keep in mind that powerful questions have an effect, whether they are answered immediately or later. When we ask powerful questions, our brains seek an answer. Depending on the question, an answer may take months or years to materialize.

A central part of cocreating something new, such as an equitable country in which multicultural relationships are valued, is living with uncertainty. Imagine letting go of a trapeze to reach for the next one. Your back may be turned away from the approaching trapeze. So it takes a leap of faith to let go of the current trapeze (a bar that is certain to keep you safe). You are cognizant that the transfer can be made only by letting go of the one certainty. Block sums it up this way:

> We want desperately to take uncertainty out of the future. But when we take uncertainty out, it is no longer the future. It is the present projected forward. Nothing new can come from the desire for a predictable tomorrow. The only way to make tomorrow predictable is to make it just like today. In fact, what distinguishes the future is its unpredictability and mystery. (p. 105)

Growth Cycles

According to Carl Rogers (1995), "what is most personal is most universal." Throughout this book we encourage inquiry as the preferred approach toward understanding the unfamiliar. Inquiry nourishes curiosity through the careful examination of personal and collective ignorance with expressed willingness to explore knowledge and expand perspective. But how do you know that you know something? This is a frequent question posed by attendees of professional learning workshops, particularly in workshops related to the idea of equity. Through our work, we have learned that educators frequently and substantially associate with inequitable references and therefore find it difficult to imagine an education system based upon fairness and justice.

Herein lies the power of reflection, which is an essential component of our awareness. It is through reflection that we come to know how we know. Humberto Maturana and Francisco Varela (1992) offer significant insight beneficial to the focus of this book:

> The moment of reflection before a mirror is always a peculiar moment: it is the moment when we become aware of that part of ourselves which we cannot see in any other way—as when we reveal the blind spot that shows us our own structure; as when we suppress blindness that it entails, filling the blank space. Reflection is a process of knowing how we know. It is an act of turning back upon ourselves. It is the only chance we have to discover our blindness and to recognize that the certainties and knowledge of others are, respectively, as overwhelming and tenuous as our own. (p. 24)

Maturana and Varela insist that it is a "crying shame" for Western culture to consider reflective inquiry as taboo and a form of active ignorance. "There are many things to be ashamed about in the world, but this ignorance is one of the worst" (p. 24).

Despite the initial feelings of inadequacy because of believing they have poor intentional reflection praxis, participants committed to advancing equity actively delve into introspective processes. Free-flowing dialogue, structured dialogue, journaling, pairing and sharing, questioning strategies, and helping trios are processes offered in this book to facilitate reflective processing.

Zig-Zags and Cycles

It is important to acknowledge reflection, knowledge acquisition, and perspective expansion. It is equally important to grasp the notion that change occurs nonlinearly because learning often transpires through iterative cyclic progressions. When entering a multicultural space, it is highly likely you will encounter new ideas and thought patterns stretching beyond the confines of your lifeworld reference. These encounters become opportunities for cyclic processing whereby you loop back upon your thinking to examine how you select data, and what you value, assume, conclude, and believe about the actions you take to construct the objective world. You will quickly identify your areas of ignorance and actively seek to understand what you do not know. Why is this important? Our premise is that the more you understand yourself, the more you will come to understand others. Furthermore, we agree with the aphorism that "you are with you always." And, as you grow and change, the greater chance that the structures around you will change.

Understanding and appreciating nonlinear growth when attending to equity speaks to maintaining an attitude of patience and perseverance anchored in peace—the greatest place of strength. When you are at peace, you can witness disturbance without being disturbed. You can make changes without feeling a sense of loss. You can confidently enter into places you once feared. You are able to receive as you give.

We share Jennifer's story as she works through cycles of reflective processing. Highly motivated, she expresses great desire to attain equitable change within her work surroundings. Consequently, she takes herself to task when tackling issues that seem beyond her reach. Her struggle to expand perspective demonstrates cycles where, at each iteration, breakthroughs are noticeable.

Jennifer's Story

Jennifer attended a five-day professional learning seminar that was hosted by her school district and facilitated by us. The goal of the workshop was to learn to use specific skills and tools to equitably respond to those you consider culturally different from yourself. Throughout the workshop, Jennifer questioned the enthusiasm her colleagues had for the process of creating authentically equitable spaces for children and families. She provided multiple examples that cast doubt as to whether a fair and just education for every student was possible. Jennifer believed that what her fellow educators espoused about inclusion was inconsistent with their behaviors of exclusion and marginalization. In fact, she raised the question of whether it was in her best interest to walk away from the educational theater. We challenged her level of commitment given that, as an adult, she had the option to walk away when her students did not. Jennifer reconsidered.

Many weeks after the workshop, Jennifer initiated a lengthy phone conversation with us in which she questioned her assumptions about engaging in equity work and expressed concern about her qualifications to do equity work because her socially assigned identity is white female. Furthermore, she questioned whether she had the level of energy needed to establish equity in her school setting. Her initial email indicates a muddied vision filled with uncertainty and captures her attempt to find clarity and focus as she rustles through her life-world references. This is a crucial phase toward perspective expansion during the initial incubation period. The question she attempts to address is *What do I bring to the context that may contribute to the current situation?*

Jennifer wrote the following:

> I work at the Spanish language immersion grade school where you cofacilitated equity training and I called you for advice last week. I write you now to express how deeply grateful I am that you took the time to speak with me. You offered several insights that I found very helpful:
>
> • Question but wait to offer suggestions. Questioning already causes some discomfort; jumping to suggestions makes it difficult for people to continue listening and reflecting.
>
> • Explain what you are doing and why you are doing it because we all should be raising questions of one another.
>
> • Instead of saying "I'd like to talk about assumptions and beliefs *before or instead of* taking action," use the word *related*. For example, "I'd like to talk about the assumptions and beliefs *related* to the action." Assume that people are willing to pause and take a look, but that they are invested in *doing* something. Asking a powerful robust question is like rewriting the script while the play is ongoing. If you try to stop the play, people stop participating.
>
> • This work takes time and often goes in cycles or zig-zags, but not a straight line.
>
> • When you don't participate, you can't effect change.
>
> I wonder if you have ever found yourself in a play that you just had to exit. I'd like to learn how to be a more effective ally. Are there particular people or authors that have influenced your thinking?

Clearly Jennifer is deeply committed to learning how to ask powerful questions. Yet, she expresses great doubt as to her ability to engage with others to advance equitable change. Her confidence suffers from her deep desire to do things the right way and a disappointment in her colleagues to authentically commit. Given that the future demands comfortability with uncertainty, what should Jennifer do? Her desire to exit the play reveals instability. Yet, it is this initial unstable phase where the greatest potential for growth occurs. The second entry bears witness to Jennifer's progression:

> It's good to hear from you; I've actually been thinking about writing you. Since the last time we spoke, I've been doing some more reading, reflecting, and have had several conversations that continue to shape my thinking.
>
> A big update that I'm excited to share with you is that I met with one of the leaders in my school district last week. In the end, the conversation went so well that the district dialogue I've been desiring to have (around our beliefs and assumptions when it comes to interacting with families) is going to happen! What's more, I get to help plan it.
>
> Right now, I'm gathering potential resources that might provide insight for that conversation. I'm asking myself how to ensure that parents' experiences and voices are represented in this conversation. I'd love to share more with you. Thanks so much for your interest. I look forward to your response, and I'll write again soon.

Jennifer aggressively absorbed additional readings, welcomed conversations, and performed self-critique to advance her knowledge about equity. These additional activities served to shape her thinking and helped her grasp ideas different from her lifeworld experience.

Jennifer has moved far beyond initial reservations about possessing abilities to learn about equity in the workplace. She readily engages in collegial critiques of policies and practices that unintentionally marginalize children and families in the school setting. She now facilitates professional learning seminars to assist colleagues who are on the path of advancing fairness and justice. She is fostering lasting equitable change.

Critical: Change in Thought

It's tempting to speed through the cycles of change when you know the critical need for the change. We've noticed that when someone searches for an immediate shift in behavior, however, a change in thinking is often overlooked. A quick fix in behavioral change does not often lead to lasting change. A change in thought processing is precisely what is needed if a sustainable shift is to transpire. Recall the Ladder of Inference (see Chapter 7) and the corresponding steps in subjective processing leading to observable objective action. It is the reflective processing, or the act of folding back on your own thinking, that leads to the possibility of reshaping outward observable behavior. It is the visible behavior in the real world that gives rise to sustainable indicators of justice and fairness. Yet, the real world is dependent on the subjective processing that shapes the way we think about how we act and behave.

As confusing as this circularity may seem, this level of processing is needed if we are to move beyond the existing state of confusion that is associated with our beliefs in the ideas of race, class, social status, sexual identity, and poverty. As we examine beliefs about our social constitution, it's clear that the objective world is prone to remain as configured if we do not change the way we *think* it ought to be. No form of legislative mandate will give rise to sustainable equitable change without a change in our hearts and minds.

Questioning with Power

Try This

It is our belief that asking questions is both an art and a skill. A powerful question can help us see something new, it can remind us of a moment in time, and it can help us understand our thoughts and bring clarity. This exercise helps you to develop a formula for asking questions. Sometimes we learn the most from the simplest words.

1. Review the highlights of this chapter.

2. Think about the following questions and comments that limit possibility and contrast those with the rephrased questions and comments that evoke possibility.

- Why does the conversation always have to be about race? *Rewritten:* In what ways might our conversations about race and culture inform us as educators and help all students to achieve at levels higher than ever before?
- Why are we held accountable for those students? They obviously don't care! *Rephrase:* What might be some of the assumptions we hold about "those" students in our community?
- Non-English speakers should all be put in another building and can join us when they can speak English. *Rephrase:* How are we adapting to students who are proficient in languages other than the language we speak?
- We need to get rid of the students of poverty. They are ruining our test scores. *Rephrase:* What four questions might you ask that, if you had the answer to, would make all the difference in the success of our students from impoverished neighborhoods? In what ways do we demonstrate our values for our families?
- This equity stuff doesn't work. *Rephrase:* In what ways might we explore schools like ours, with students and families (demographics) like ours, that are successfully working in equitable ways?

3. Record the sorts of inequitable questions and comments that you hear—and recast them or write response questions.

4. Role-play the questions or comments with trusted family and friends. Your role is to respond with questions that evoke possibility. Take the conversation wherever it goes.

5. Practice. Practice. Practice!

Think about and rephrase the questions and comments that limit possibility and contrast those with questions and comments that evoke possibility.

Try This

Rephrasing Questions and Comments

Practice rephrasing comments and questions that limit possibilities to questions that evoke possibilities. A few examples are listed. Try adding a few comments from your recent experiences, and work with a colleague, trusted friend, or family member to rephrase them. With practice, we expect you will be able to evoke possibilities easily.

- A staff member says to a student, "Why are *you* using the gender-neutral bathroom?"
- A staff member says to another staff member (who speaks with an accent), "You need to work on your English pronunciation."
- My department chair asked me to do equity work but didn't tell me how. How can I do a task when administration provides no resources?

Appendix:
Extension Experiences

You may never know what results come of your action,
but if you do nothing, there will be no result.
–Mahatma Gandhi

Throughout this book, we provide many opportunities for you to apply what you've learned. We encourage your continued exploration by providing these additional exercises. Our intent is for you to practice what you've learned because we believe it is one thing to inspire and nurture the *will* to engage with others, but it is our belief that practice is necessary to develop the *skill* to do so. Without practice, the *will* often begins to fade.

We begin this section by sharing Jennifer's exciting news. She created a Try This exercise specifically for her group of family and friends in which she practiced questioning skills using a provocative 20-minute video clip. We share her experience as a way of encouraging you on the journey toward advancing equity through conversations that move beyond race, class, and culture.

> I did it.... I had eight people over yesterday evening. We were able to divide into pairs and into two groups of four, yet the whole group was small enough for people to feel comfortable sharing their stories and experiences. In two hours, it was possible for everyone to contribute.

Inevitably, one group did not follow the Final Word protocol that I learned in one of your workshops. (I gave directions but didn't model it.) In the group that used the protocol, two people were less likely than others to speak up. The protocol worked well for one person, but not our member who is learning English as a Second Language (ESL). That person had difficulty following the conversation and dealing with the pressure of speaking at a prescribed time or at all.

Afterward, I talked with him and asked what I might do differently to help anyone crossing borders. He didn't have immediate ideas but we talked about code switching, which he agreed might help if it were being done for more than one person.

Another participant admitted being uncomfortable asking questions when it meant pointing out a difference between or among members. That felt rude, she said. I asked her where she had learned that pointing out a difference was uncomfortable or rude. She replied that as an engineer she wants to blend in—and not have people point out the obvious difference (she's female). Another person agreed, indicating that she didn't want to be treated differently when she was working in the male-dominated technology field.

"I just wanted to feel equal," my friend said.

"So, I think I hear you saying that pointing out a difference draws attention to something that is unequal," I said, "And you find that uncomfortable or rude. Is that right?" (That was my attempt to clarify or paraphrase.)

Later, I realized that the crux of our ESL member's experience seemed to be about blending in, too. Moving past the discomfort of pointing out differences is something my group may be interested in exploring next.

Our hope is that you, too, can put our guidance into action to help improve your skills for engaging in deeper conversations. You can use these exercises as practice and can add them to your repertoire. Each activity is labeled with the chapter number that corresponds most closely with the content.

Chapter 1

Examining Our Identity

As we become aware of our cultural identities, we can begin to explore how we experience different aspects of our identity. We also notice how others might experience us. In other words, how people see us and how we see ourselves can be significantly different. We also know that there is more to each of us than what other people see. We all have stories of joys, challenges, tragedies, and struggles. Our stories are often kept to ourselves or stowed beneath our surface of what we share with others. The following activity is designed to help us share ourselves and see more clearly what lies beneath the surface of our fellow human beings.

1. Self-reflect and record your response to the following prompts:
   - When people look at me, they see _____.
   - If they really knew me, they would see _____.
2. Share your answers with a trusted friend, family member, or colleague. Ask your friend to self-reflect, record, and share answers to those questions.
3. Together, reflect on the experience using these questions.
   - What feelings came up for you when you shared your reflection?
   - What are you learning about yourself?
   - How might this experience influence future interactions?
   - How was this experience meaningful?

Adapted from Krownapple, J. (2016). Guiding teams to excellence with equity [Workshop]. Vancouver, BC, December 3, 2016.

Exploring Our Labels

We have many dimensions to our identity. The simplest way to explain who we are or how others might see us is through our use of social labels, such as white, single, gay, or Native American. Sometimes labels bring us joy and sometimes they bring us pain. Follow these steps to explore the labels with which you self-identify or are used by others to identify you.

1. Choose a trusted friend, colleague, or family member to do this exercise with you.

2. Work independently by writing your name on a piece of paper and recording the different labels or cultural identifiers that might be used to define you, such as a citizen of the United States, female, educator, athlete, Greek Orthodox, middle-aged, overweight, farmer, and widow.

3. Take turns sharing a memory related to one cultural label that you associate with pain or sorrow.

4. Take turns sharing a memory related to a cultural label that you associate with joy or that puts a smile on your face.

5. Have a reflective conversation with your trusted friend that is guided by these questions:

- What feelings did you experience when you shared your memories or stories?
- What are you learning about yourself and the trusted person?
- How might this experience influence future interactions with others?
- What are you learning about labels and their effects?
- How was this experience meaningful?

Chapter 2

Using Common Language

Having language in common is essential to participation in a public space.

After reading and reacting to the list of definitions provided in Chapter 2, consider if you or your community uses any other terms that need clarity or rethinking.

1. Make a list of the terms you would like to better understand. List your working definition, your experiences related to it, and related questions. Here's an example, using the term *ableism*:

- Record your working definition. *Negative value applied to the extent to which a person is able to complete a task physically or intellectually.*
- What are your experiences with this term?
- What questions do you have about this term? *How does this word differ from* disabled?

2. Share your words with a trusted friend, colleague, or family member. Ask that person to share how he or she experiences the term. Check for agreement of the definition. If you disagree, begin to discuss what it would take to create a mutually agreed-upon definition.

Try This   Seeking to Understand Values

Values are deeply held views of what we consider to be important. Most of us learned our values from a significant person in our life, such as a parent, guardian, uncle, or person who raised you. Values are influenced by many sources, including religion, schools, peers, and people we admire. Be mindful that there's a distinction between what we say we do and what we actually do. Espoused values are those that we *say* we believe and values in use are what we actually *do* (our actions). Certain circumstances can cause us to act in ways that are incongruent with two deeply held values. For instance, we may espouse that we value honesty and relationships, but we may be dishonest to spare someone's feelings (a polite lie) and preserve a relationship. When we act congruently with our values, however, we experience less stress in our lives. Although questioning our values may generate dissonance, it allows us to better understand our culture as well as the culture of others and facilitates cross-cultural communication.

When working with groups of people, it is important to agree on definitions of terms, general or specific, that are or will be used in the discussion. If we can create shared definitions for our conversations, they can help us to better understand the dynamics of diversity. Seeking to understand, instead of seeking to debate, allows us to broaden our horizons. Because culture is comprised of values and beliefs that have become normalized, we ask you to explore ways of creating definitions around value systems.

We offer a list of values to help you start with this exercise. We encourage you to add others that are important to you.

1. Identify two trusted family members, colleagues, or friends.

2. Each of you should identify three values that are most important to you. (Don't expect this to be easy.) Circle your top three:

Accomplishment	Exciting activity	Optimism
Accountability	Faith	Perseverance
Adaptability	Fame	Personal best
Attention to detail	Family	Privacy
Authentic	Fitness	Reflection
Being right	Fitting in	Relationships
Belief in higher power	Freedom	Reliability
Candor	Friends	Religion
Cleverness	Generosity	Respect elders
Collectivism	Hard work	Responsibility
Commitment	Health	Revenge
Common sense	Healthy eating	Risk-taking
Communication	Honesty	Rule follower
Consistency	Hope	Safety
Cooperation	Humility	Sarcasm
Courage	Humor	Self-discipline
Creativity	Individualism	Self-reliance
Curiosity	Innovation	Self-respect
Decisiveness	Intelligence	Separate but equal
Dependability	Intuition	Service
Diversity	Justice	Social skills
Earnest	Kindness	Societal status
Ecology	Knowledge	Spirituality
Economic security	Leadership	Stewardship
Education	Learning	Tolerance
Effectiveness	Living within means	Tranquility
Efficiency	Meditation	Truth
Emotional security	Morals	Vulnerability
Equality	Music	Wisdom
Equity	Obedience	
Ethics	Open-mindedness	

3. As a group, share your values using the following questions to guide your conversation:

- How do you define each value?
- From whom did you learn each value?
- How do you call on these values to make decisions?
- How do these values present themselves at home? At work?

4. As a group, identify one value that you share.

- How do each of you define the value for yourself?
- What does it look like in action?
- Take turns sharing your responses.

5. Select one member as a recorder and work together to create a shared definition of the value. Agree upon ways in which you can hold yourself and each other accountable for living by the value. Check in with each other in a few weeks to share examples of using this value in your lives.

Chapter 3

Focusing on Listening and Feedback

Sometimes there is more to what is being said than the words that are spoken. And, of course, listening and observing is a huge factor in effective communication. In this activity, you'll need five participants (four plus you).

1. Identify and enlist four trusted friends, family members, or colleagues.

2. Assign roles for the first round.

- Participant 1: Storyteller talks about a situation that is important to him or her.
- Participant 2 listens for feelings connected to the story.
- Participant 3 listens for expressed values.
- Participant 4 listens for the substance in the story.
- Participant 5 acts as facilitator and reminds everyone to stay focused on the assigned role, keeps track of time, and records feedback to give to the listeners (see 4).

3. When the storyteller finishes, the participants take turns sharing information from their focus area. The storyteller confirms or denies each set of feedback. The round might sound like this:

- Participant 2 (feelings): It sounded like you were feeling frustrated when your car wouldn't start. Is that correct?
- Participant 1 (storyteller) response: No, that isn't correct. I was scared because I was alone and didn't know what to do.

4. Share and provide feedback in rounds. The number of rounds is determined by the number of participants in the group. Here are the steps.

- (5 minutes) Storyteller shares a situation of personal importance. Other members of the group listen according to their assigned focus areas (feelings, expressed values, content).
- (10 minutes) As participants 2, 3, and 4 share the information they gathered in their roles, the storyteller (only) responds briefly by confirming or denying the information, as in the example shared in 3.
- (5 minutes) Facilitator provides feedback in the form of questions to the participants. For example, "How might your eye contact affect the storyteller?" or "How might your tone of voice affect the storyteller or listener?"

5. Repeat the process and assign different focus areas and roles until each participant has experienced each role.

6. Use these questions to guide your reflection.

- Did the structure help or hamper your ability to listen?
- What are you learning about yourself as a listener?
- What should you attend to when listening to others?

Overcoming Fears

Try This

Engaging in fierce conversations can be challenging. Emotional states motivated by fear can freeze our decision-making ability. To avoid freezing up in difficult situations, we need to face and practice overcoming these fears.

1. Record your fears as they relate to engaging in fierce conversations. Common examples range from fear of being misunderstood to fear of offending the person you're talking with. Start by listing three fears you have about difficult conversations.

2. Brainstorm ideas, including behaviors, that will help you overcome fears that prohibit your engagement in a fierce conversation. For example, "I need to remember to breathe when I speak to others" or "I need to build my skill through the practice of asking powerful questions."

3. Use the template to start exploring your fears and engaging in critical conversations:

- What is the challenge?
  - _____

- Of what are you afraid?
  - _____

- After the conversation, record how you felt about the experience.
  - _____

Here are examples:
- What is the challenge?
  - Sharing my feelings
- Of what are you afraid?
  - I am afraid that my feelings will be rejected or ignored.
- After the conversation, record how you felt about the experience.
  - I tested this by sharing with a friend a time that he really hurt me. I was surprised that I expressed my emotions in a clear way. I did get a little emotional when sharing. I could hear my voice shake and feel my hands sweat. My friend didn't dismiss my feelings; in fact, he asked how he could repair the relationship.

4. Keep a personal reflection journal. Each time you notice a fear surfacing, acknowledge the fear, lean into the challenge, and then reflect on the conversation. Soon your reflection journal will serve as a reminder of the fears that you have worked through, and it can become your inspirational journal.

Chapter 4

Listening with Your Head, Heart, and Feet

Strengthening listening capability requires space for purposeful practice, proper feedback, and critical reflection. You'll need about an hour and five participants (including yourself).

1. Gather four trusted friends, colleagues, or family members. You will act as facilitator.

2. The other participants will experience each role during different rounds. There is a storyteller and three listeners for each round.

- Storyteller: Share a situation, reflection, or reaction that is weighing on your heart.
- Participant 1 focuses on the **head**, logic, and common sense thinking in what the storyteller is sharing.
- Participant 2 focuses on the **heart**, or the feelings or emotions in what the storyteller is sharing.
- Participant 3 focuses on the **feet**, or the motivation and willingness of the participant in what the storyteller is sharing.

3. Use the following structure to manage the time in each round.

- Storyteller shares a story (5 minutes).
- Each participant responds with elements of the story focused on the assigned role (head, heart, and feet). As the facilitator, check to see that what is said aligns with what the storyteller shared. Each listener shares for about 3 minutes each (9 minutes).
- After listening to all the feedback from the listeners, the storyteller gives feedback to the listeners (2 minutes). The feedback might sound like the following:
  — You were right on target with my feelings.
  — I am curious as to what words or body language gave you clues about my motivation.
  — When you were nodding your head, it distracted me from what I was sharing.

Repeat this process until each person has an opportunity to experience each role.

Note: The idea for this exercise was inspired by http://organizationunbound.org/expressive-change/listening-to-the-head-heart-feet/

Paraphrasing

Try This

Practice paraphrasing independently or with a partner. When paraphrasing, it is important to acknowledge, clarify, and summarize what you heard with the anticipated result of increased understanding. Increasing your understanding of others and communicating more fluently is the intent of this practice.

Set aside potential distractions and commit to fully listening.

1. Record one of your favorite television shows or movies.

2. In a comfortable space, view five minutes of the recording. As you are watching the performance and listening to the dialogue, make mental notes of the words spoken.

3. Pause the recording and get ready to paraphrase. Do not simply repeat what was said ("What I heard you say was _____") but capture the essence of the message from the main character. Below are examples of how you might paraphrase what the character conveyed:

- You are feeling frustrated because she left you alone.
- You are wondering if you will ever get out of debt.
- It sounds like you are going to seek support from your family.
- You are thinking about exploring your options.

4. Replay the recording and check to see how you did. Were you able to acknowledge, clarify, and summarize what was said?

5. Repeat as many times as you would like or until you are comfortable paraphrasing what the character said.

6. Extend this skill development by practicing with a trusted friend, family member, or colleague. After you have paraphrased a conversation, ask them for feedback.

- What was it like for them to have you paraphrase the conversation?
- Did you capture the essence of what they said?
- Did they feel heard?

Chapter 5

Practicing "Thank you"

Sometimes it is difficult to accept positive feedback with the simple but powerful response: thank you. Many of us tend *not* to think about our strengths (nor do we share or celebrate them). We tend to think about what we need to improve upon rather than affirm what we do well, which makes it difficult for us to accept even a mere acknowledgment of our strengths. During this exercise, we encourage you to *lean into* accepting declarations of your strengths.

1. Gather four to five trusted friends, colleagues, or family members. Give each person a piece of paper, a pen or pencil, and 20 small self-adhesive mailing labels. Instruct each person to write his or her name in the center of the sheet of paper and put it aside.

2. Ask each person to think of something he or she views as an accomplishment. It might be a time in which he or she overcame a challenge or achieved a goal. Allow five minutes for silent reflection.

3. Ask each person to tell the story in five minutes (uninterrupted). During the storytelling, the other members of the group write a one-word descriptor of the person's strength on a label. (The word describes the storyteller's character, given the accomplishments shared.)

4. At the conclusion of each story, each listener makes eye contact with the storyteller and makes a short remark about what is written on the label. The label is then placed on the storyteller's paper. For example, if the label is "courageous," the participant may say, "Frank, I see you as courageous for standing up to your colleagues with what you thought was right."

Repeat the process until each person has shared a story and received labels or notes from the group.

5. Use the following questions to guide reflection about this experience.

- What did you think, feel, or wonder while you were sharing your story?
- What did you think, feel, or wonder as you offered the strengths to other people?

- What did you think, feel, or wonder as you received the feedback of strengths?
- What implications does this have for working relationships with students? Community? Colleagues?

Lindsey et al. (2018), p. 208.

Prepping for Difficult Conversations

Engaging in difficult yet critical conversations conjures emotions, and not all are likely to be positive. Difficult conversations are viewed as perilous and risky and may invoke fear, guilt, shame, anger, anxiety, or frustration. These emotional states act as conversation paralyzers, jeopardizing the information exchange needed to maintain and nurture healthy relationships. Yet, we need to have these critical conversations to advance equity—and we can improve our ability to have these conversations with proper reflection and practice.

1. Think of a person with whom you want to or need to have a critical conversation. Think of why you need or want to engage with this person. Ask yourself the following questions and record your thoughts.
   - With whom do you want to have a critical conversation?
   - Why is it important to have this conversation? What is the value?
   - What makes this a critical (dangerous, perilous, or risky) conversation?
   - What is your biggest fear about engaging in this conversation? Perhaps think about what the worst outcome might be.
   - What strengths will you summon?
   - What are the essential logistics for having this conversation? Time? Location?
   - What are your hopes for moving forward or through this conversation with this person? What do you expect or hope to accomplish by having this conversation?
   - What do you have invested in this relationship that gives you the confidence to critically engage?

2. Develop a plan for having the conversation. You may wish to use the following ideas and sentence starters to guide your thinking.

- What is the purpose of the conversation?
  - — I want to talk with you because _____.
- Identify the perceived "wrong."
  - — When you did or said _____.
- Explore feelings.
  - — When you _____.
  - — I felt _____.
- What questions do you have?
  - — What was your intent?
  - — How did I contribute to this perceived "wrong"?
- What would it take to repair this relationship? What would it take to right the perceived wrong?
  - — How can we repair this?

3. Implement your plan. Get comfortable with being uncomfortable. Envision yourself engaged in the conversation and reflect on the possible effects your words might have on the other person. In front of a mirror, practice making eye contact and talking about the problem. You may use a sentence starter such as "I want to talk with you because _____. When you _____, I felt _____." Be aware of what your body language communicates to the listener. Practice will bolster your confidence in having a positive conversation.

4. Now that you have carefully thought about, prepared, and rehearsed what you want to say, it is time to have the conversation. Up to this point, only you know if you will have the critical conversation. Seize the opportunity—summon your courage, step into the spotlight, and expose the conflict.

5. After the conversation, reflect on the experience. Think about the good things that came out of the conversation, consider the conversations that might need to happen in the future, think about your feelings, and reflect on what you might do differently for the next tough conversation.

Chapter 6

Thinking About Our Differences and Context

People can experience the same environments in different ways. Consider how others might describe different situations or circumstances. Places, people, gatherings, seasons, home purchases, jobs, and education may be good topics to use as you explore the differences in perceived realities. The same place or experience might evoke a wonderful, joyful memory from one person and sadness from another.

1. Choose three trusted friends, colleagues, or family members to interview. These people should be perceived as different from you in race, gender, sexual orientation, social-economic class, age, or lived experience.

2. Privately interview each person for about 30 minutes. With permission, take written notes and record it electronically. Do not share your notes with anyone else. All note taking is for your personal review and reflection. Destroy all notes within two weeks to preserve confidentiality.

3. In each interview, ask the person to help you to explore differences in your life experiences. Remember to use the ground rules for the discussion in Chapter 2 and the dialogic strategies discussed throughout this book.

4. Use the following questions for the interview, and feel free to add other questions. The purpose of this interview is to gain insight into how you and others might have different experiences in the same environments. For example, I might have a belief that because we work in the same environment, our experiences are the same.

- Tell me about a time when you have experienced being "different."
- When have you felt connected to a group?
- When have you felt disconnected from a group?
- What have you learned about yourself and how you respond to others?

5. At the conclusion of each interview, reflect on the following questions.

- What moments were most vivid, good and bad, as we engaged in this interview?
- What feelings arose during our interview?
- What did we learn from this interview?

6. After you have interviewed your trusted friends, colleagues, or family members, and you have reflected personally on that experience, share with them how you have been affected. Below are a few sentence starters to help you.

- When you shared _____, it made me feel _____.
- I want to thank you for sharing _____ because _____.
- As a result of you sharing _____ it made me think of _____.
- After hearing your story, I am _____.

Try This

Reflecting on a Timeline of Differences

Our daily interactions, along with the choices we make and our thoughts about others, affect how we experience the world. Big events and little moments influence us. This activity asks you to recall events in your life in which you experienced or realized differences—including factors of diversity (such as ability level, race, family structure, sexual orientation, economic class, and religion).

1. Think about times when you were affected by diversity. When did you become aware of the diversity around you? Record your thoughts.

2. Gather materials to create a diversity lifeline—a personal work of art. You might need markers, crayons, pens, magazine clippings, stickers, and a large piece of paper to create your masterpiece. Use pictures, dates, locations, and captions to tell your story. You are documenting your life, as it relates to when you experienced differences. The differences that you document could include those related to age, gender, religion, culture, and traditions. Enjoy the process.

3. Share your masterpiece with a trusted friend, colleague, or family member. Tell your story. Encourage your trusted friend, colleague, or family member to ask questions about your masterpiece. Encourage them to create a masterpiece of their own.

4. Reflect on your experience of making and sharing your timeline of differences. Use these prompts to get started.

- What was it like to reflect on your life, as it relates to equity?
- What are some moments that struck you as important?
- What are you learning about yourself and your response to difference?
- How might this learning influence your future interactions with colleagues, community members, students, families, and strangers?

Lindsey et al. (2018), p. 184.

Chapter 7

Living Up to Expectations

Try This

When exploring the *beliefs* step on the Ladder of Inference, we are also exploring the expectations that we have for ourselves and others. To explore those expectations, consider your deepest held beliefs: *Do you believe in someone's abilities as that person expresses them, or do you hold beliefs about what you think that person can do?*

The answer is understanding how you come to know what you think you know. Are you able to change your mind and shift your belief about someone? Can you refocus your mind to see something you have not seen before? Can you help someone see something "new" or special in himself or herself? Advancing equity charges you with formulating questions as you pursue the realization of a more civil society.

1. Think of a student, friend, acquaintance, colleague, or family member with whom you would like to have a better relationship. Refer to this person as Person A (for ease of reference). Keep in mind that this exercise will not change Person A, but it is designed to help *you* change the way you perceive and respond to the person. On a piece of paper, write Person A's strengths, unique abilities, capabilities, and positive character traits.

2. Share the list with someone you choose as a discussion partner—without identifying Person A.

3. Use the following prompts to talk about this experience.

- What was it like for you to record positive strengths, abilities, and capabilities about Person A?
- How is it to share those words out loud?
- What are implications for your relationship with Person A, based upon this experience?
- When you interact with Person A, will you take the opportunity to respond using the lens of the newly created positive characteristics from this experience?

4. Afterward, journal about what the discussion felt like and how your discussion partner responded to you.

Try This

Trading Assumptions

Practice applying the imagery of the Ladder of Inference to experience moving through the steps and then reflect on that experience. We know that moving up and down the steps of the Ladder of Inference happens quickly. Slowing the process strengthens the capacity to harvest what was learned. To do this activity, you'll need to recruit a partner.

1. Choose someone you do not know well—perhaps a casual acquaintance from work or from your neighborhood—to take part in this exercise. Find a comfortable yet quiet and inviting space. Allow 30 minutes.

2. In silence, each of you should write what you perceive to be the correct answers about the other person. (Your perception is your best guess about the person sitting across from you.)

- Where the person grew up
- Country of family origin and heritage
- Language(s) spoken
- Religion
- Interests or hobbies
- Favorite foods
- Preferred type of movies or TV programs

- Preferred type of music
- Pets, if any, or favorite animals

3. After recording your answers, take turns sharing. After each answer, share the correct information with each other.

4. Talk about this experience. Use the prompts below to guide your conversation.

- Which assumptions were accurate? Which were not?
- Why did you make the assumptions about your partner? For example, you assumed or thought your partner only speaks one language because most people you know speak only one language. Or, "My partner likes dogs because I have seen her with dogs in my neighborhood."
- How did it feel to have the responsibility for making assumptions?
- How did it feel to be the recipient of assumptions?
- What insights does this give to the act of stereotyping?
- How does this experience help you make sense of the Ladder of Inference?

Adapted from Lindsey et al. (2018), p. 214.

Chapter 8

Questioning Your Questions

Exhibiting authentic curiosity and wonder, often signaled by powerful and insightful questions, helps us to develop meaningful and mindful relationships. Begin this exercise by thinking about the type of questions you typically ask in a critical conversation. Also, consider when and where you are most likely to pose these sorts of questions. Contemplate the intent of the questions. Do they seek to surface and examine a value, assumption, or belief? Will your questions untangle a conclusion or help you to scrutinize the foundation of a tightly held belief? Understanding your intent for asking questions can help you to develop thoughtful, deep, meaningful inquiries that strengthen relationships.

1. Set up a table to record the type of questions you may have asked in a previous difficult conversation. Consider conversations from hallways, classrooms, gas stations, supermarkets, or community gatherings.
2. Make a list of the questions that you've asked.
3. Code each question by marking an *X* in the appropriate column.
4. Notice the types of questions you generally ask (open-ended, yes or no, answers implied in the question). We've coded some examples of open-ended questions to help guide you.

Question	Assumption	Value	Belief	Context	Conclusion
What predictions are you making about us regarding our same-sex marriages and families?	X				
What is most important to teach to students in your class?		X			
What principle guided you to have a child removed from your classroom?			X		
Where were you when you realized that the principle, which guided a child's removal from class, was important to you?				X	
Why are you certain that some children are gifted and others are not?					X

5. Use these prompts to guide your reflection:
   - Did your question match your purpose for asking the question?
   - What type of questions were easy for you to ask?
   - What type of questions were more challenging for you to ask?
   - What are you learning about yourself as it relates to asking questions?
   - How might this influence your future interactions with others?

Source: Adapted from *Better Conversations: Coaching Ourselves and Each Other to Be More Credible, Caring, and Connected*, Jim Knight, 2016. Thousand Oaks, CA: Corwin. Used with permission.

Using Your Imagination

Profound questions are inspired by curiosity. The simple desire to know about someone or something is fundamental to human development, interaction, and progress. You will need your imagination and a childlike innocence for this exercise.

1. Think of a current or historical figure with whom you would like to have a conversation. Imagine having this conversation in a casual setting, such as around a dinner table. Choose any figure, but here are a few ideas: Chinua Achebe, Susan B. Anthony, Cesar Chavez, Red Cloud, Alexander Hamilton, Delores Huerta, Nelson Mandela, Mother Teresa, Eleanor Roosevelt, Amy Tang, and Leonardo da Vinci.

2. Develop questions to ask. Focus on open-ended questions because you are curious to understand the thinking behind his or her work. Powerful questions create a window into what a person thinks and believes. Here are a few ideas that may help you develop potentially powerful questions:

What you want to know: What beliefs undergird how and why you took action?

- Dr. King, what principles did you draw upon to prepare and deliver the "I Have a Dream" speech in Washington, DC?
- Delores Huerta, what values guided your actions as you led the Chicano movement?
- Mother Teresa, what assumptions did you make that caused you to conclude that caring for the sick and poor was the right thing to do with your life?

3. Now that you have created questions to ask someone in an imaginary setting, invite someone who is actually in your life to have coffee to ask them powerful questions about their life experiences.

4. Use these prompts to guide your reflection about the conversation.

- What did you learn about yourself when you were asking questions?
- What did you learn about your invitee?
- What was easy about this process?
- What was difficult about this process?
- Why was this experience meaningful?

References

Argyris, C. (1990). *Overcoming organizational defenses: Facilitating organizational learning*. Boston: Allyn & Bacon.

Baldwin, C. (2005). *Storycatcher: Making sense of our lives through the power and practice of stories*. Navato, CA: New World.

Bellinger, G. (2004). *Knowledge management-emerging perspectives: Systems thinking*. Available: https://thesystemsthinker.com/author/gene-bellinger/

Blankstein, A. M., & Noguera, P. (2016). *Excellence through equity: Five principles of courageous leadership to guide achievement for every student*. Alexandria, VA: ASCD.

Block, P. (2008). *Community: The structure of belonging*. San Francisco: Berrett-Koehler.

Bohm, D. (1999). *On dialogue*. New York: Routledge.

Brookfield, S. (2005). Learning democratic reason: The adult education project of Jurgen Habermas. *Teachers College Record, 107*(6), 1127–68.

CampbellJones, B. (2002). *Against the stream: White men who act in ways to eradicate racism and white privilege/entitlement in the United States of America*. [unpublished doctoral dissertation]. Claremont, CA: Claremont Graduate School.

CampbellJones F., CampbellJones, B., & Lindsey, R. (2010). *The cultural proficiency journey: Moving beyond ethical barriers toward profound school change*. Thousand Oaks, CA: Corwin.

Caron, C. (2018, May 9). Yale police are called over a black student napping in her building. *New York Times*, p. A21. Available: https://www.nytimes.com/2018/05/09/nyregion/yale-black-student-nap.html

Carson, C., & Holloran, P. (1998). *A knock at midnight: Inspiration from the great sermons of Reverend Martin Luther King, Jr.* New York: Warner Books.

Courage. (n.d.). In *Merriam-Webster's collegiate dictionary*. Retrieved from http://www.merriam-webster.com/dictionary/courage

Covey, S. M. (2006). *The speed of trust: The one thing that changes everything*. New York: Free Press.

Cross, T. L. (1989, March). *Towards a culturally competent system of care*. Washington, DC: Georgetown University Child Development Center.

Delpit, L. (1995). *Other people's children: Cultural conflict in the classroom*. New York: New Press.

Ellinor, L., & Gerard, G. (1998). *Dialogue: Rediscovering the transforming power of conversation.* New York: Wiley.

Ferguson, R. (2003). Teachers' perceptions and expectations and the black-white test score gap. *Urban Education, 38* (4), 460–507.

Freire, P. (2000). *Pedagogy of the oppressed.* New York: Continuum.

Freire, P., & Shor, I. (1987). *Pedagogue of liberation: Dialogues on transforming education.* Westport, CT: Bergin & Garvey.

Gadamer, H. G. (1991). *Plato's dialectical ethics: Phenomenological interpretations relating to the Philebus.* New Haven, CT: Yale University Press.

Gladwell, M. (2005). *Blink: The power of thinking without thinking.* New York: Little, Brown.

Gorski, E. F. (2008). *Theology of religions: A sourcebook for interreligious study.* Mahwah, NJ: Paulist Press.

Grissom J. A., & Redding, C. (2016). Discretion and disproportionality: Explaining the underrepresentation of high-achieving students of color in gifted programs. *AERA Open, 2*(1), 1–25.

Habermas, J. (1990). *Moral consciousness and communicative action.* Cambridge, MA: MIT Press.

Heidegger, M., Macquarrie, J., & Robinson, E. S. (1968). *Being and time.* New York: Harper.

Heifetz, R. (1994). *Leadership without easy answers.* Cambridge, MA: Belknap Press.

Herda, A. (1999). *Research conversations and narrative: A critical hermeneutic orientation in participatory inquiry.* Westport, CT: Praeger.

International Center for Transitional Justice. (2018). Home page. https://www.ictj.org/about

King, M. L., Jr. (Speaker). (1998). *A knock at midnight: Inspiration from the great sermons of Reverend Martin Luther King, Jr.* Cassette Recording.

Knight, J. (2016). *Better conversations: Coaching ourselves and each other to be more credible, caring, and connected.* Thousand Oaks, CA: Corwin.

Krownapple, J. (2017). *Guiding teams to excellence with equity: Culturally proficient facilitation.* Thousand Oaks, CA: Corwin.

Ladson-Billings, G. J. (2016). And then there is this thing called the curriculum: Organization, imagination, mind. *Educational Researcher, 45*(2), 100–104.

Larson, C. E., & LaFasto, F. M. (1989). *Teamwork: What must go right/What can go wrong.* Newbury Park, CA: Sage.

Lathrap, M. T. (n.d.). "Judge softly" or "Walk a mile in his moccasins." Available: https://jamesmilson.com/about-the-blog/judge-softly-or-walk-a-mile-in-his-moccasins-by-mary-t-lathrap/

Lewis, O. (1961). *The children of Sanchez: Autobiography of a Mexican family.* New York: Random.

Lindsey, D., Lindsey, R., Nuri-Robins, K., Terrell, R. D., & Diaz, R. M. (2013). *A culturally proficient response to LGBT communities: A guide for educators.* Thousand Oaks, CA: Corwin.

Lindsey, D. B., Jungwirth, L. D., Pahl, J. V., & Lindsey, R. B. (2009). *Culturally proficient learning communities: Confronting inequities through collaborative curiosity.* Thousand Oaks, CA: Corwin.

Lindsey, R. B., Nuri-Robins, K., Terrell, R. D., & Lindsey, D. B. (2018). *Cultural proficiency: A manual for school leaders* (4th ed.). Thousand Oaks, CA: Corwin.

Lindsey, R. B., Roberts, L., & CampbellJones, F. (2013). *The culturally proficient school.* Thousand Oaks, CA: Corwin.

Madsen, S. R., Gygi, J., Hammond, S. C., & Plowman, S. F. (2009*). Forgiveness as a workplace intervention: The literature and a proposed framework.* Peru, NE: Institute of Behavioral and Applied Management.

Maturana, H. R., & Varela, F. J. (1992). *The tree of knowledge.* Boston: Shambhala Publications.

Northouse, P. G. (2019). *Leadership: Theory and practice* (8th ed.). Thousand Oaks, CA: Sage.

Owens, R. (1995). *Organizational behavior in education* (5th ed.). Boston: Allyn & Bacon.

Phillip, P. (2016, December 14). 1.7 million people in 33 states and D.C. cast a ballot without voting in the presidential race. *Washington Post.*

Robert, A. H. (1998). *Mastering the art of creative collaboration.* New York: McGraw-Hill.

Rogers, C. (1995). *On becoming a person: A therapist's view of psychotherapy* (7th ed.). New York: Mariner Books.

Schein, E. (2004). *Organizational culture and leadership* (3rd ed.). San Francisco: Jossey-Bass.

Schein, E. H. (1984). Coming to a new awareness of organizational culture. *Sloan Management Review 25*(2)3–14.

Scott, S. (2004). *Fierce conversations: Achieving success at work and in life, one conversation at a time.* New York: New American Library.

Senge, P. M. (1990). *The fifth discipline: The art and practice of the learning organization.* New York: Doubleday.

Senge, P. M., Kleiner, A., Roberts, C., Ross, R., & Smith, B. (1994). *The fifth discipline fieldbook.* New York: Doubleday.

Sergiovanni, T. (2001). *The principalship: A reflective practice perspective* (4th ed.). Boston: Allyn & Bacon.

Shultz, H. (2018, May 19). *An open letter to Starbucks customers from executive chairman Howard Schultz.* Retrieved from https://news.starbucks.com/news/an-open-letter-to-starbucks-customers-from-howard-schultz

Siegel, R. (2018, May 3). Two black men arrested at Starbucks settle with Philadelphia for $1 each. *Washington Post.* Retrieved from https://www.washingtonpost.com/news/business/wp/2018/05/02/african-american-men-arrested-at-starbucks-reach-1-settlement-with-the-city-secure-promise-for-200000-grant-program-for-young-entrepreneurs/?utm_term=.0a9bab5e7abf

Singleton, G. E. (2015). *Courageous conversations about race* (2nd ed.). Thousand Oaks, CA: Corwin.

Singleton, G. E., & Linton, C. (2006). *Courageous conversations about race.* Thousand Oaks, CA: Corwin.

Sleeter, C. (2005). *Un-standardizing curriculum: Multicultural teaching in the standards based classroom.* New York: Teachers College Press.

Takaki, R. (1993). *A history of multicultural America.* New York: Little, Brown.

Tatum, B. D. (2017). *Why are all the black kids sitting together in the cafeteria? And other conversations about race.* New York: Basic Books.

Thompson, G. L. (2018). *The power of one: How you can help or harm African American students.* Thousand Oaks, CA: Sage.

Thompson, K. (2009, July 21). Harvard scholar Henry Louis Gates arrested. *Washington Post*. Retrieved from http://www.washingtonpost.com/wp-dyn/content/article/2009/07/20/AR2009072001358.html

Weick, K. (1979). *The social psychology of organizing* (2nd ed.). New York: McGraw Hill.

Wenger, E. C., & Snyder, W. M. (2000.) Communities of practice: The organizational frontier. *Harvard Business Review*, 139–145.

Whack, E. H. (2018, May 3). Black men arrested in Starbucks settle with Philadelphia for $1 each, plus $200K for youth. *USA Today*. https://www.usatoday.com/story/news/nation/2018/05/02/black-men-arrested-starbucks-settle-philadelphia-entrepreneurs/573470002/

Wheatley, M. J. (2009). *Turning to one another: Simple conversations to restore hope to the future*. San Francisco: Berrett-Koehler.

Index

Note: The letter *f* following a page locator denotes a figure.

About the Authors

 **Dr. Brenda CampbellJones** is president of CampbellJones & Associates. She provides professional learning and technical assistance to school districts throughout the United States and Canada. Brenda has served as a teacher, an elementary principal, an award-winning middle school principal, an area superintendent, and a university professor. As regional director of the California School Leadership Academy, she led the staff development efforts for 33 school districts. Brenda coaches and facilitates the change process in school districts that are making systemic changes for student academic and social achievement. She is coauthor of the best-selling book *The Cultural Proficiency Journey: Moving Beyond Ethical Barriers Toward Profound School Change*. Brenda may be contacted at www.campbelljones.org.

 **Shannon Keeny** specializes in supporting schools, offices, and communities to effectively engage in conversations that help explore access, fairness, and belongingness in the educational environment. Shannon's passion drives her to honor each person's lived experience by creating space in which we can all learn and grow. Immersed in this work for more than a decade, the core of her efforts is ensuring that people are valued, accepted, and honored. Shannon has served the educational community as a teacher

and facilitator for the Howard County (Maryland) Public School System and adjunct professor at McDaniel College. She presents at national and international conferences. Shannon may be contacted at shanlk719@aol.com.

Dr. Franklin CampbellJones works closely with schools and educational systems in the United States and Canada to ensure establishment and maintenance of equitable learning environments for children. His life's work includes service to education as a high school social science and reading teacher, school administrator, district office director, and state director for the California School Leadership Academy. Franklin was also professor of education leadership at CSU Los Angeles, Rowan University, and Towson University. His books include *The Culturally Proficient School: An Implementation Guide for School Leaders, The Cultural Proficiency Journey: Moving Beyond Ethical Barriers Toward Profound School Change,* and *Journey of Spirit, Walk of Faith: Our Relationship with God.* Franklin may be contacted at www .campbelljones.org.

Related ASCD Resources:
Equity, Culture, and Critical Conversations

At the time of publication, the following resources were available (ASCD stock numbers in parentheses).

Becoming a Globally Competent Leader by Ariel Tichnor-Wagner (#119011)

Becoming a Globally Competent Teacher by Ariel Tichnor-Wagner, Hillary Parkhouse, Jocelyn Glazier, and J. Montana Cain (#119012)

Becoming the Educator They Need: Strategies, Mindsets, and Beliefs for Supporting Male Black and Latino Students by Robert Jackson (#119010)

Building Equity: Policies and Practices to Empower All Learners by Dominique Smith, Nancy E. Frey, Ian Pumpian, and Douglas B. Fisher (#117031)

C.R.A.F.T. Conversations for Teacher Growth: How to Build Bridges and Cultivate Expertise by Sally J. Zepeda, Lakesha Robinson Goff, and Stefanie W. Steele (#120001)

Cultural Competence Now: 56 Exercises to Help Educators Understand and Challenge Bias, Racism, and Privilege by Vernita Mayfield (#118043)

Excellence Through Equity: Five Principles of Courageous Leadership to Guide Achievement for Every Student by Alan M. Blankstein, Pedro Noguera, with Lorena Kelly (#116070)

Motivating Black Males to Achieve in School and in Life by Baruti K. Kafele (#109013)

Raising Black Students' Achievement Through Culturally Responsive Teaching by Johnnie McKinley (#110004)

Teaching Boys Who Struggle in School: Strategies That Turn Underachievers into Successful Learners by Kathleen Cleveland (#111028)

Your Students, My Students, Our Students: Rethinking Equitable and Inclusive Classrooms by Lee Ann Jung, Nancy Frey, Douglas Fisher, and Julie Kroener (#119019)

For up-to-date information about ASCD resources, go to www.ascd.org. You can search the complete archives of *Educational Leadership* at www.ascd.org/el.

ASCD myTeachSource®
Download resources from a professional learning platform with hundreds of research-based best practices and tools for your classroom at http://myteachsource.ascd.org/

For more information, send an e-mail to member@ascd.org; call 1-800-933-2723 or 703-578-9600; send a fax to 703-575-5400; or write to Information Services, ASCD, 1703 N. Beauregard St., Alexandria, VA 22311-1714 USA.

WHOLE CHILD
TENETS

The ASCD Whole Child approach is an effort to transition from a focus on narrowly defined academic achievement to one that promotes the long-term development and success of all children. Through this approach, ASCD supports educators, families, community members, and policymakers as they move from a vision about educating the whole child to sustainable, collaborative actions.

Culture, Class and Race relates to the **healthy, safe,** and **engaged** tenets. *For more about the ASCD Whole Child approach, visit **www.ascd .org/wholechild.***

1 HEALTHY
Each student enters school healthy and learns about and practices a healthy lifestyle.

2 SAFE
Each student learns in an environment that is physically and emotionally safe for students and adults.

3 ENGAGED
Each student is actively engaged in learning and is connected to the school and broader community.

4 SUPPORTED
Each student has access to personalized learning and is supported by qualified, caring adults.

5 CHALLENGED
Each student is challenged academically and prepared for success in college or further study and for employment and participation in a global environment.